THE PROGRESSIVE'S GUIDE TO
RAISING HELL

How to Win Grassroots Campaigns, Pass Ballot Box Laws, and Get the Change We Voted For

JAMIE COURT

CHELSEA GREEN PUBLISHING
WHITE RIVER JUNCTION, VERMONT

Project Manager: Patricia Stone
Developmental Editor: Joni Praded
Copy Editor: Cannon Labrie
Proofreader: Nancy Ringer
Designer: Peter Holm, Sterling Hill Productions

Printed in Canada
First printing August, 2010
10 9 8 7 6 5 4 3 2 1   10 11 12 13

Our Commitment to Green Publishing

Chelsea Green sees publishing as a tool for cultural change and ecological stewardship. We strive to align our book manufacturing practices with our editorial mission and to reduce the impact of our business enterprise in the environment. We print our books and catalogs on chlorine-free recycled paper, using vegetable-based inks whenever possible. This book may cost slightly more because we use recycled paper, and we hope you'll agree that it's worth it. Chelsea Green is a member of the Green Press Initiative (www.greenpressinitiative.org), a nonprofit coalition of publishers, manufacturers, and authors working to protect the world's endangered forests and conserve natural resources. *The Progressive's Guide to Raising Hell* was printed on Legacy Natural, a 100-percent postconsumer recycled paper supplied by Webcom.

Library of Congress Cataloging-in-Publication Data
Court, Jamie, 1967-
 The progressive's guide to raising hell : how to win grassroots campaigns, pass ballot box laws, and get the change we voted for / Jamie Court.
  p. cm.
 Includes bibliographical references.
 ISBN 978-1-60358-293-3 (alk. paper)
 1. Political participation--United States. 2. Direct democracy--United States. 3. Politics, Practical--United States. 4. Progressivism (United States politics) I. Title.

JK1764.C68 2010
323.4'40973--dc22

2010027448

Chelsea Green Publishing Company
Post Office Box 428
White River Junction, VT 05001
(802) 295-6300
www.chelseagreen.com

ANCIENT FOREST™ FRIENDLY

Preserving our environment
Chelsea Green Publishing chose to print the pages of this book on recycled paper and saved these resources[1]:

	energy	water	greenhouse gases	solid waste
40 trees were saved for our forests	44 million BTUs	64,016 gal.	13,292 lbs	3,997 lbs

Printed by Webcom Inc. on Legacy Hi-Bulk Natural 100% post-consumer waste.

FSC
Mixed Sources
Product group from well-managed forests, controlled sources and recycled wood or fiber
Cert no. SW-COC-002358
www.fsc.org
© 1996 Forest Stewardship Council

[1]Estimates were made using the Environmental Defense Paper Calculator.

Additional Praise for Jamie Court and His Previous Books

"A tireless consumer activist."
—*Los Angeles Times*

"Pamphleteers like Thomas Paine and Thomas Jefferson awakened their compatriots to the injustices suffered under King George III, and perhaps it will be author-activists like Court who help us again declare our independence and assert our sovereignty."
—*San Francisco Bay Guardian*

"Upton Sinclair would be proud."
—**Jim Hightower, national radio commentator and author of** *Swim Against the Current*

"Jamie Court shows how, in dimension after dimension, corporateering has become both ball and chain on America's promise and an implant within our consciousness. It's time to become self-conscious before the large corporations achieve their ultimate merger—with you! Are you skeptical? Read Jamie Court. A star is born."
—**Ralph Nader**

"He's notorious for his dramatic, sharp-tongued attacks on the health-care and auto-insurance industries, and on any politician who takes their campaign cash."
—*The Wall Street Journal*

"Jamie Court is one activist health maintenance executives love to hate."
—*San Francisco Chronicle*

". . . Jamie Court shows how . . . everyday 'corporateering' springs from the same assumptions and strategies that led to the fire sales on stock at Enron, Global Crossing, WorldCom, and so on. This book teaches you how to see the invisible hand of the corporation, and the finger is pointing at you."
—**Michael Moore, activist filmmaker, from his foreword to** *Corporateering*

Previous Books by Jamie Court

*Corporateering: How Corporate Power Steals Your
Personal Freedom . . . and What You Can Do About It*

Making a Killing: HMOs and the Threat to Your Health
with Francis Smith

THE PROGRESSIVE'S GUIDE TO

RAISING HELL

For Joey and Pablo, the greatest hell-raisers in the world, and Michelle, who works selflessly and tirelessly every day to build a more just world

CONTENTS

ACKNOWLEDGMENTS

My wife and partner, Michelle Williams Court, has given her unwavering support and counsel day in and day out for my advocacy and projects for twenty years, even when it comes at her own personal peril. Her generous insight, courage, compassion, and experiences flow through every campaign and page in this book.

My friend Jeremy Tarcher and I first discussed this book about seven years ago. He has selflessly nourished and developed the project with his keen insight, expansive mind, and provocative questions.

My mentor and friend Harvey Rosenfield is a hell-raiser's hell-raiser. His courage, creativity, and idealism continue to inspire all of us at Consumer Watchdog daily. His support, teaching, example, and friendship made this book and its lessons possible.

Consumer Watchdog's dedicated and talented staff prove every day that a small group of committed people can make all the difference. Doug Heller, Pam Pressley, Jerry Flanagan, Judy Dugan, John Simpson, Carmen Balber, and Todd Foreman take on the biggest corporations in America. They win through the force of their passion, creativity, and hard work. Each has contributed his or her experiences and insight to this book. Internet director Kent McInnis has greatly enriched the text with his views about online activism. Mark Reback and Carmen Aguado are the indispensable support team behind all of Consumer Watchdog's efforts. I am grateful for the opportunity to work with such committed individuals and in awe of their example.

Consumer Watchdog board members Kathy Olsen, Ellen Snortland, and Chic Wolk have each inspired me based on their personal journeys. Their collective support allowed me the necessary time to complete this project. My allies at the California Nurses Association are the best friends a hell-raiser could have. I am thankful for the friendship of the mighty union, the most progressive in America, and its leader Rose Ann DeMoro. My friend Michael Lighty has generously offered his wisdom and comments for this book.

My agent Stu Miller took on this project out of conviction, and his astute perspective has shaped both the text and its publication. He has gone above and beyond the call.

Finally, the team at Chelsea Green has my gratitude for bringing this project to life on such a short timeline. Margo Baldwin saw the need to reinvigorate progressives. Joni Praded enlivened the book with her deft editing and progressive vision.

INTRODUCTION

I'm asking you to believe. Not just in my ability to bring about real change in Washington. . . . I'm asking you to believe in yours.

—BARACK OBAMA

President Franklin Delano Roosevelt is said to have told progressive activists, after listening to their proposals, "I agree. I am all for your plan. Now make me do it." The premise of *The Progressive's Guide to Raising Hell* is that it is now the job of average Americans to make the president, Congress, and state government officials live up to the reform they promised.

Strange as that may sound, public-interest advocates hear "make me do it" all the time. Regulators ask to be sued so they will have to issue the consumer protection rules they know they need to write. Governors and attorneys general want to be petitioned so that they can answer. Legislators ask us to file state ballot measures so that they can get a state legislature to act before the public does. It's not that good regulators, statewide officials, or legislators don't want to respect the law and public opinion, it's that they cannot do it in the system we have without a well-articulated popular mandate. Like an honest and diligent president, they know they represent us, but we have to show them, and those who surround them, that there's no way out in a representative democracy. We are them. They embody us. They have to act.

President Barack Obama faces more pressure from Tea Party activists than from his base. This must change if anger is to move America forward, rather than turning back the clock to a time when government was a symbol of oppression. For the founders of our nation, and for progressives today who seek to better the lot of average Americans, government is an expression of our collective will, storied history of self-determination, and highest hopes.

Obama's first anniversary in office fell on the day after he lost his supposedly filibuster-proof supermajority in the Senate. Insurgent

Republican Scott Brown, with an injection of energy from the antigovernment Tea Party movement, won the U.S. Senate seat held by Ted Kennedy and Democrats for five decades in the most Democratic state in the nation. The president acknowledged that the same anti-establishment sentiment that had swept him into the White House one year earlier had bitten him back. Anger, not hope, had given Obama the job, and it could take it away.

During his first year, Obama had given in to the Wall Street bankers, the war hawks in Afghanistan, the oil companies, and the medical insurance complex, not to mention the cash-and-carry politicians of his own party who occupied key positions in Washington but would not budge on the president's top priorities. Americans watched a record bonus season at the taxpayer-rescued Wall Street banks, but they didn't see any of the spoils. All the public got was 10 percent unemployment, near zero interest on their savings, and 15 percent interest on their credit cards. Health reform turned into a Frankenstein. The outsider in the White House had capitulated to the insiders, and his party paid a price.

Obama's failures during his first year had de-energized his progressive base and had likely cost Brown's opponent, Democrat Martha Coakley, the race that she was originally thought sure to win. The message was that the president needed to tend to his people and deliver, taking a tougher stand with Wall Street and Washington and not trying to be everyone's friend. One day after the Massachusetts election Obama endorsed a tough banking reform, finally adopting former Federal Reserve chairman Paul Volker's call to restrict deposit-taking, FDIC-insured banks from operating hedge funds and private equity funds or engaging in other risky speculative investments that put their depositors' funds in danger.

Two days after the Massachusetts special election, the U.S. Supreme Court delivered a shocking ruling—in *Citizens United v. Federal Elections Committee*—that ended the six-decade-old ban on direct corporate political contributions. With populist fervor reminiscent of FDR, Obama vowed to move Congress to challenge the court and prevent corporate money from buying elections.

Whether Obama can ultimately deliver on his renewed promises, however, is not as important as whether the public learns that it has the power to make change happen. Americans don't need to wait for an election, or for Obama. What the public needs is a plan.

Creating such a plan, powered by citizens, may seem daunting—even more so now that the Supreme Court's Citizens United ruling has opened up American politics to unlimited amounts of corporate campaign cash. Every little-guy group and David vs. Goliath candidate will need a different strategy, a new form of leverage, to fight money with truth. My twenty years of experience in populist guerrilla politics offers some lessons about how this can be done right.

After the 2008 election, my small California group, Consumer Watchdog, invested in a second location—a storefront Washington, D.C., office at Fourth and East Capitol Street—and sent our best young organizer out to change the world. We did this with the knowledge that change would not come in the usual ways that Americans expect, from the top down. We had few illusions about the president giving us all that had been promised on the campaign trail, although we believed he would use his platform and his knowledge to better effect. We strapped in for the long haul with the understanding that all change is about opportunity, and waiting for, or creating, a window to make it happen. This book explains how to move when the window's open.

Turning Anger into Change

Change is no simple matter in American politics, as Americans have recently learned so well. Elections rarely produce the change they promise because too often ballot victories leave intact the ways power is exercised, and on whose behalf. The special interests that fund and curry favor with our legislators may rebalance their party allegiances, but not their self-interest.

After the vote, power vacuums fill with familiar values, if not faces. Promises give way to fiscal realities, hope succumbs to pragmatism, and ambition concedes to inertia. The old tricks of interest groups—

confuse, diffuse, scare—prevail over the better angels of American nature.

President Obama made some major missteps during his first year in office, including betraying some key campaign promises, but this book is not about Obama's errors. It's about how populist energy can get change making and change makers back on the right track.

Anger, not hope, is the fuel of political and economic change. As things grow worse and worse, public rage grows more intense—and so does the energy for making things better. And in 2010 in America, anger rules, but it needs to be vectored and focused if it is to succeed in fueling the type of change that the majority of Americans believe in. If progressives walk away, rather than engage, the Tea Party and GOP will capture the popular anger and turn it against government, rather than focusing it rightly back on the targets of the 2008 election: Wall Street, health insurers, polluters, the military industrial complex, and the politicians they buy. If we want progress, the kind that polls show 60 percent of Americans believe in, we need to do more than vote every two to four years or wait for Obama to learn the tactics of confrontation.

So how can we get what we believed we voted for?

In the pages ahead, you'll find a road map that answers that question by building on these few simple truths that have the power to catalyze change.

1. Public opinion is the most powerful force in the world. While it can be muted, distracted, and co-opted, it cannot be controlled, except by the public.

2. Americans need to understand exactly how special interest groups and politicians play on their fears and distract them. Lack of this fundamental understanding is, more often than not, the reason populist campaigns for change fail.

3. The vast majority of Americans do want sweeping changes to guarantee that they have real, affordable health care coverage, financial regulation, and access

to cleaner, cheaper energy, and the old bogeymen can be overcome with the right strategies and unflinching tactics.

4. Politicians rarely lead; it's too politically risky. The public leads, and politicians follow.

If you believe, as I do, that these truths are evident, then the tactics, strategies, and assumptions of this book have a chance to succeed. Together, we need only apply them and spread them.

The difficult times we now face have changed America and Americans, but not the American political establishment. It may take a president, Congress, or statehouse to help, but they are not the engines of change. We are—average Americans, everyday citizens. And it's time to start the motor.

The fundamental premise of this book is that change relies on popular opinion and the power and will of opinion leaders to mobilize the public around it. Americans may understand the power of cash-rich special interests to foil their greatest hopes for change, and even some of the tactics those interests groups use to maintain the status quo. They have far less understanding of their own power as a people to influence and create the change they agree upon.

President Obama's key failure in his first year was turning his back on the opinions of the public that elected him. He gave too much to the well-heeled industries and entrenched politicians when he could have fought them straight up with the public on his side. What Obama failed to realize was that, win or lose in his first year, he would then have created a record and a movement that ultimately succeeded. Losing a battle when you stand on principle helps you gather followers and amass the power to one day win the war.

The hope that politics as usual would spur real change from the White House was clearly a mirage. *The Progressive's Guide to Raising Hell* proposes a vision and foundation for "politics-as-unusual." It's not for politicians, who will never lead, but for the people, who must show elected leaders what their demands are.

When populism works, particularly progressive populism, it can be infectious. By recounting battle stories of progressive populist successes, and the tactics that catalyzed them, I want to show Americans how real change is still possible and how its possibility rests entirely upon their knowledge of the rules of engagement and ability to act when it counts.

The Right Time to Act

Having hope may be a lot more audacious today than when Obama was elected, but the power of government has never been more in the American people's hands, through technology and political circumstance. There has not been a greater anticorporate or anti–Wall Street climate in modern American history. Populists and progressives can prevail by playing the same hardball as status-quo insiders.

Opportunities exist in two key arenas—online and at the state level. Online, Obama vacated the populist pulpit he occupied during the election, leaving room for populist reformers to seize the platform and harness its energy. At the state level public opinion can focus on outrages and solutions that are closer to home, and politicians are more vulnerable to their own mistakes and hubris. The ballot-initiative process in twenty-four states and the District of Columbia, which allows citizens to propose laws for voters to approve, also offers the possibility, and the threat, of direct democracy. Health reform, for instance, will be progressive when implemented only if states improve upon the new federal law signed by Obama in March.

Federally, the time has come for major game changers. The abuse of the filibuster by a retrenched minority in the U.S. Senate is begging for a recalculation or an elimination of the rule that calls for sixty votes to defeat a filibuster—nine more than would ordinarily pass a bill. Many major Democratic funders are refusing to open their wallets for U.S. Senate candidates until they pledge to eliminate the rule or reduce the sixty-vote margin, which can be done by a simple majority vote of the Senate. The public needs to take up the call.

Similarly, the Supreme Court's rule of unlimited corporate campaign contributions will face its public backlash too, be it unprecedented transparency or a major revision of the legal role of corporations in American life. Combine this with massive restlessness over the economy, the wars, and capitulations to the oil industry, and it's easy to understand why anger might have ripened enough to provoke action.

The long and proud history of our nation is that when tyrants overreach, the American people unite to set them straight.

As I write this, many Americans may no longer believe in President Obama's ability to bring about real change in Washington. This book offers a blueprint for wresting opportunity from discontent, so that we can make the president—and the rest of the political establishment—"just do it."

Jamie Court
Los Angeles. CA

CHAPTER ONE

THE ART OF CHANGE

I love my job. I hate politicians and the cash-register politics that defines our political system. Every day I get to do what I love: change what I hate.

There are those who believe political change can only be bought, with big checks delivered to politicians and their pet causes. Based on our successes, my colleagues and I at Consumer Watchdog, where I've advocated in the public interest for a decade and a half, know there is another way—a simple formula for creating change that does not involve making campaign contributions.

The power of public opinion is what creates change. Issues move politicians, not the other way around. Change is within Americans' grasp, if they understand their own power and how to focus and leverage it.

The public can win if its opinion is focused like a beam, and if the right person with a platform holds up a lens at the right time to magnify the force of the public's light.

Sure, big money can distract the public or distort the information we receive. Big campaign checks also do buy fine print in laws, line items in budgets, political appointments. In the end, though, public opinion can prevail over the richest and most powerful people and interest groups, when that opinion is strong and focused enough.

Exposing pressing social issues, harnessing the energy of public opinion, and waiting for windows of opportunity to open have occupied the past two decades of my life. The organization I head, Consumer Watchdog, works with other public interest groups to enact all manner of reforms in California and around the nation. My colleagues and I were able to pioneer HMO reforms in forty-four states, regulate insurance companies, beat Big Oil, tame Goliaths like Arnold Schwarzenegger, and depose some of the most corrupt politicians in the nation. The record we created against abuses by health insurance companies spurred the most progressive parts of President Obama's health insurance overhaul.

Our strategy has been to show powerful people and companies how out of touch they are with popular values. Those who grasp the message, and change, survive. Those who resist often dig their own political graves.

The majority of Americans, not just full-time reformers, can also make their opinions count daily, in simple ways that assert their political power and reinforce their vote.

To fully understand how, follow me back to the fall of 2007, and to a meeting with a few guys who deliver big political checks and a powerful politician who received them. All of them had the wrong idea about how things work.

Change Comes from the Outside

A few months before the 2008 presidential primaries began to really heat up I found myself in a Beverly Hills hotel penthouse suite across from a co-chair of Hillary Clinton's campaign: the speaker of the California Assembly, Fabian Núñez. The second most powerful politician in the state wasn't happy.

A mutual acquaintance, a billionaire movie producer, had set up the face-to-face. As another Consumer Watchdog supporter, Warren Beatty, told it, the speaker had had a little too much red wine at a small dinner party and started ranting about my consumer group and me. The billionaire who lived in the penthouse, a chief Hillary Clinton supporter, wanted me to sit down with Núñez and some of his key dinner companions from that evening to set the record straight. Beatty, a champion of Consumer Watchdog's reform efforts and someone we've recognized for his public service work, suggested that it might be a good idea.

The producer had a record of putting his money where his mouth is, supporting progressive and green causes. We had worked together on projects, including successful opposition to Governor Arnold Schwarzenegger's slate of reactionary ballot measures to reshape California government to the detriment of progressives and those they care about in 2005. I thought he understood that my colleagues and I always spoke our minds, regardless of whose friend or candidate was at issue.

Consumer Watchdog had been vocal in criticizing a luxury junket Speaker Núñez and his wife had taken to South America, where he spent time with Chevron's lobbyist. The trip was paid for by an energy foundation funded by the oil company and other energy producers. Afterward, the speaker took in fifty grand in political contributions from Chevron and torpedoed bills to reform the oil companies.

Núñez's friends had told him that he should hear me out and try to settle our disputes.

This was exactly the type of meeting I had avoided for a decade and a half as a consumer advocate. My strategy had been to stay on the outside. My general rule of political engagement is that change is inspired from the outside, not from within. Forget the seat at the table; find the rock to throw through the window. But I felt I had an opportunity. Núñez still could undo some of the damage he did to oil-industry reform. He also was about to make a monumental choice on health care reform.

Governor Schwarzenegger wanted Núñez to endorse the notion of requiring every Californian to show proof of health insurance, which meant having to buy it. Núñez had initially listened to those of us who said that without regulating insurance companies, the price would be too high for most California families. But news reports had suggested Núñez was about to side with Schwarzenegger—essentially trading his support on the mandatory health insurance for the governor's support on a ballot initiative that would extend political term limits. The ballot initiative was Núñez's pet project. If it failed, Núñez and many of his allies would be without a job in a year. If it succeeded, he would have six more years in office.

I also knew that Núñez's position on the mandatory purchase of health insurance could ultimately reflect that of Senator Clinton, at the time still the presumptive Democratic presidential nominee, who had yet to articulate her health care plan. I wanted to stop that presidential train wreck before it started.

The speaker started off the penthouse meeting on exactly the wrong foot. He said he was glad we were getting together, that he thought that the people in the room were some of my donors, and that it was important that I be accountable, too. He objected to my group's sharp criticism of his South American junket. He argued that unlike some people in the room he couldn't afford his own private jet to see ethanol factories in Brazil, so he had to rely on others to pay. Núñez claimed our criticism was simply a personal attack and that we needed to "spread it around." Then the speaker said that the only justification he could see for our action was "racism."

I had brought my colleague Judy Dugan, who after twenty years on the *Los Angeles Times* editorial board came to our group to raise hell. She had seen everything, or so she thought. She—and others in the room like Beatty—knew my wife is African American and my two children were adopted from Central America.

Núñez had walked into the room with one of the nation's wealthiest trial lawyers, Tom Girardi. Friends call Girardi a "lawyer without peer," largely because he bankrolls so many great cases, like the one that led to the case portrayed in the Erin Brockovich movie. In the courtroom, he represents the little guy against the rich and powerful. In politics and business, where he owns a big stake in casinos, he is considered a titan. Girardi set John Edwards's senatorial and presidential campaign in motion before turning his support to Hillary Clinton. He reportedly owned a twelve-passenger Gulfstream IV jet, or "G-4." Girardi's chumminess with Núñez told me that they had taken a few flights together. During Núñez's tenure, the legislature gave casino owners new freedom from the previous prohibition preventing the ownership of gambling enterprises inside and outside of California.

The penthouse group understood and believed in the power of money and influence. Many of their progressive values reflected my own on issues like the environment, consumer rights, and corporate accountability. What separated us was the notion of how change occurs.

They believed in insider connections, political machinery, and the money that greased both. To them, it was just a question of which team, red or blue, would marshal its resources and get there first. They were the blue squad. For me, genuine change has always been born of an uncontainable populism that knew no party. Perhaps that's why I was as frank as I was when my turn came.

I handed the speaker a stack of letters we had written him in the past year about his legislation on gasoline prices, health care, telecommunications, and political accountability. I said that if he had answered one of the letters, perhaps we wouldn't be where we were. Then I explained our philosophy. No matter who is in or out of the room, we call it as we see it because our credibility is all we have. I reminded Núñez that the only reason he was paying attention to us was that we had embarrassed him in the media. Otherwise he would have continued to ignore us because we didn't give political contributions. That's what we do, I said. We show powerful people how out of touch they are with the people they claim to represent, to force them to change. That's why, I said, I had similar conversations with the last four speakers of the assembly. We weren't about to change; it was he who needed to.

You could tell that not many people had talked to Núñez that way since he had become speaker. Núñez accused me of being too negative, unrealistic, and harsh. I pointed out that his actions triggered our reactions. Only after he took Chevron's side on oil-company regulation did we point out the campaign contributions he solicited from Chevron. Only after he undermined one of our modest health-insurer reform bills did we criticize the $50,000 he took from Blue Cross for a fund-raiser at the soccer World Cup final. And only after AT&T coughed up six figures to sponsor the "Speaker's Cup" golf fund-raiser at Pebble Beach for Núñez did we take a close look at his telecommunications deregulation effort, whose main beneficiary was AT&T.

Núñez claimed we had different views on what was good for the consumer. I said I agreed. We certainly didn't believe stripping away even meager government oversight of cable TV and telephone companies was good for society.

The back-and-forth turned to the governor's plan for mandatory private health insurance purchases and Schwarzenegger's refusal to regulate the industry to make sure that people could afford to pay the premiums. This turned out to be the very debate that Barack Obama and Hillary Clinton would have six months later in the heat of the primary. Obama won by opposing mandatory health insurance purchases, taking on the populist view, but later reversed himself during his first year in office. It was one of a series of betrayals on health care reform during Obama's first year that undermined his support among his progressive base and independents.

In the penthouse, Núñez and I lost the rest of the group on the details of the public policy in play, but the debate was healthy. Núñez ultimately insisted that he came from humble roots, his dad was a janitor, and he would never force people to pay for private health insurance they couldn't afford. I made it clear that if he reneged, that would be the arena of our dispute. We agreed to try to work together. Núñez even made a show of calling his staff on the spot to try to work out some of our smaller disagreements.

Leaving, I doubted we had really changed his mind. Sure enough, a month or so later, Núñez endorsed Schwarzenegger's mandatory private health insurance plan. The insurers would get to charge what they wanted, and the middle class would have to pay. Núñez announced in the assembly's health committee, "We don't regulate the health insurance industry," a statement that came back to haunt him. Not long after that, the governor reversed his earlier stance and endorsed Núñez's term-limits extension ballot measure.

What befell Núñez after he threw middle-class families to the insurance company wolves neither he nor anyone else in that room could have predicted.

Núñez had always presented himself as a working-class champion, which was one reason his support for mandatory insurance was so valuable to Schwarzenegger. We had been among the first to raise the issue of his overseas junkets, and his appearance of pay-to-play politics. Eventually, the *Los Angeles Times* printed a report that made that image indelible.

Public records showed Núñez had been spending extravagant amounts of his campaign contributors' money on global jet-setting, including a $2,500 spree at Louis Vuitton, $5,000 at a swank Bordeaux wine shop, and thousands at one of the ritziest hotels in Barcelona. Worse, Núñez's response was to literally run away from the news cameras, making for an infamous television clip of the speaker being chased down a hallway by reporters.

We had already made it a public issue that Núñez took in more campaign contributions from insurers than any other legislator. That, combined with the damage to Núñez's working-class credibility and motives, was a major factor in stopping Schwarzenegger's mandatory insurance legislation in its tracks.

Núñez's jet-setting scandal also became the basis for television commercials against the speaker's ballot measure on term limits. Voters shot down that initiative even though special interest groups with business before the legislature spent $11 million trying to keep Núñez in office. The day after the election Núñez's colleagues began jockeying to replace him as speaker. His final salvo was that he had no regrets and that racism was the cause of his demise. Among the speaker's last words in that post: "Because of the fact I am a Mexican, they think I have to sleep under a cactus and eat from taco stands."

Núñez's arrogance, denial, and blindness to his own vices became the seeds of his own defeat. After the *Los Angeles Times* story broke, Girardi, the lawyer, purportedly became enraged with what had happened to Núñez and, ultimately, term limits. He bad-mouthed our consumer group to others in the G-4 set. What really angered Girardi, according to those close to him, was a mass e-mail communiqué Consumer Watchdog sent out just before the election, opposing the term-limits initiative and pointing out, as a reason for that opposition, the top donations to Núñez's effort. Along with a big-business and big-union roster, it included $225,000 from Girardi's law firm.

It's always been astonishing to me that those who rely on money for their power, particularly for campaign contributions, become so enraged when anyone makes mention of it. Put out a press release about a politician's campaign contributions and you become a pariah of the capitol. For that sin, I've been dressed down by billionaires and politicians from governors to U.S. senators. They say money doesn't buy political favors, it's simply an expression of support.

To me it's all chicken and egg. The point is that the public doesn't approve of a special interest group or rich donor with a stake in a policy debate financing the decision makers. What if a judge took payments or junkets from the parties in a case she was overseeing? The public doesn't want the number one state legislator living large across the globe on his campaign contributors' credit card. When you're going against the big guns of money in politics, public opinion is the A-bomb.

It turns out the public also doesn't want to be forced by the government to pay for a health insurance policy that is unaffordable. That's how the record we created with Núñez and Schwarzenegger on the health insurance issue landed us in the middle of the 2008 presidential campaign.

Getting National Politics Back on Track

When Hillary Clinton first endorsed mandatory health insurance, Matt Lauer, host of the *Today* show, confronted her on air with a quote of mine that had appeared in *Newsweek*. I had made the comment a week before she announced her position, hoping to head her off from supporting mandatory health insurance.

> **Matt Lauer:** Let me read you something that Jamie Court told *Newsweek* magazine. He said, "There's nobody in this race with her knowledge to make health care available to every American at a cheaper cost, but it would take going after the insurance industry that's funding her candidacy." In fact, some of your competitors have said you have taken more money from the insurance industry than any other candidate,

so is conflict looming on the horizon? Are you losing
leverage in asking these insurance companies to get on
board and make tough choices?

Hillary Clinton: Well, I don't think so because I believe
in reality-based politics.

Clinton made the comment well before the first Iowa Caucus,
at a time when she was the clear front-runner. Her "reality-based"
politics later handed her a third place in Iowa and began the loss of
momentum that led to her campaign's ultimate demise. In the 2008
presidential primary battle over who would be the real agent of
change, the old-style Clinton triangulation just didn't cut it.

Barack Obama, whose campaign my colleagues and I never talked
to, used our talking points, almost verbatim, to attack Clinton's
mandatory purchase plan. At the time no one in America was making
the same arguments in the same way as Consumer Watchdog was.
California was on the cutting edge of the debate, and some of my
arguments in a *Los Angeles Times* op-ed about the parallel to mandatory auto insurance laws later became the basis for Obama campaign
statements. Obama said, "The reason people don't have health insurance isn't because they don't want it, it's because they can't afford it."
Obama had a platform. We had a populist message. The public had
a strong opinion that turned out to be a defining difference in who
became the Democratic nominee.

Flash forward to January 2010, Obama's one-year anniversary in
the Oval Office. To win moderate Democratic support for health
reform legislation, President Obama had months before agreed to
mandatory health insurance purchases for every U.S. citizen, the very
kind of "reality-based" politics he had criticized Hillary Clinton for.
He also jettisoned from the legislation the so-called public option to
the private health insurers, another key campaign plank. Even earlier
in his presidency he had cut a deal with pharmaceutical companies
not to subject them to new government bulk purchasing that would
lower prescription drug costs in exchange for the industry's support
for health reform legislation. The populist campaigner had given in

to every cash-rich industry in the health care reform debate so as not to incur their wrath. While he railed against the power of money in Washington on the campaign trial, he bowed to the big-money donors at pivotal moments once he occupied the Oval Office. These critical turning points not only guaranteed that health care reform, as written by Congress, would not be cost-effective, but confirmed for the watchful public that Obama was not an authentic reformer. Quickly, the public bit back in Massachusetts on January 19, 2010, when the special election to fill the U.S. Senate seat vacated by Ted Kennedy's death suddenly turned into a referendum on Obama's leadership. The Massachusetts electorate, which had more independents by 2010 than either Democrats or Republicans, took away the Democrats' supposed filibuster-proof majority in the Senate. Obama Democrats stayed home, while a strong turnout of Republicans and a swing contingent of independents gave Scott Brown the edge.

Those who study politics look for such tipping points because they understand that momentum is the key force in politics. The GOP proved it could disguise itself as outsiders and retake power. The White House would have to get back in touch with the people or pay a price.

Is there a way to get Obama back on track? How can Americans get the change they want when the politicians who represent them are either too corrupted by big money or too scared of it to represent them as an outsider would? The Senate special-election vote in Massachusetts showed the public's patience had run short, but its anger has yet to be quelled. How can populist anger be used for more than punishing unpopular politics and politicians in elections? How and why do populist campaigns succeed beyond candidate elections?

Rich or not, Americans tend to invest their hope for change in change makers. That's the nature of elections—and that's why the public's hope turns to despair when a perceived change maker like Obama fails. But there is an alternative to candidate-driven politics, and it's a proven route to change.

The American people pay more attention to elections than the process of making change itself. Consequently, the public often won't see when the process is on target or gone awry. That robs them of their great power, which is knowing when and how to focus the force of their opinions. The greatest weapon at the disposal of the enemies of popular change is distraction. The greatest asset of populist change makers is the public's focus. That's why the war over public opinion is the most significant part of any policy or political battle in America. It's not just politicians but interest groups of every stripe that have pollsters, perception managers, and crisis management specialists trying to tap into popular ideas in order to spin their concepts and positions.

Campaigns for change against powerful opponents like the insurance industry can succeed when public opinion is fully focused behind them, particularly when they are based on strong moral principles. These campaigns define leaders who buy into them, not the other way around. The exploits of my Consumer Watchdog colleagues and I over the last two decades offer important lessons for Americans looking at how to get the change they voted for.

When HMOs tried to throw newborns and their mothers out of the hospital only hours after a birth in order to save money, we mobilized Congress to stop them. Not only did we succeed, but a good number of politicians saw their careers soar because they took up the cause. When industry bureaucrats tried to tell doctors what was "medically necessary," we passed new laws to prevent the second-guessing. After the companies refused to pay for second opinions, our campaign made the HMOs pay up. Officials who joined with us became public heroes.

A decade earlier, California's property-casualty insurers succumbed to the strongest regulations in the nation after my consumer group's founder, and my mentor, Harvey Rosenfield, rallied public opinion. Harvey led a ballot measure revolt, via his insurance reform Proposition 103, that has saved California motorists more than $62 billion on their premiums according to a 2008 Consumer Federation of America report. For two decades California politicians' allegiance to insurance regulation has defined their success in state politics. We taught the insurance companies and others in the Fortune 100, as well as the politicians who work for them, a lesson through practical steps that muster and focus public opinion to turn the tables on injustice. Our political allies profited more from standing with the public than from pandering to an industry's checkbooks.

The campaign for California Proposition 103 in 1988 has particular relevance for America now. The "voter revolt" of 1988 was sparked by mandatory auto insurance laws imposed by California's legislature without any requirement that insurance be affordable for those who had to buy it. The populist ballot measure required insurance companies to seek approval for premium hikes from the state insurance commissioner, a post Proposition 103 made an elected position, before raising premiums. It also rolled back excessive rates and delivered $1.43 billion in refund checks to consumers, ended zip-code-based auto insurance, and subjected the industry to antitrust restrictions. The two dozen states with ballot-measure processes offer Americans a similar opportunity to rein in private health insurers now that a national discussion of their vices has been aired, and mandatory, private health insurance will be the law of the land in 2014.

The Five Steps

In each of Consumer Watchdog's campaigns, regardless of whether it was for a ballot initiative or another measure of public opinion, my colleagues and I faced familiar hurdles in moving from one phase to another, and we faced similar tactics from our opponents. In all the campaigns the arguments, phases, and tactics in the art of creating change and in the craft of foiling it are remarkably similar regardless of what the issue is.

Here are the five steps necessary for any campaign to succeed at creating change.

Step 1: Expose. Exposing new information about opponents—facts that conflict with the image they put forth in public—shows how out of touch with public opinion those opponents are.

Step 2: Confront. Confronting our opponents on the battle-ground of our values creates a debate, an unfolding drama, over popular values through which a campaign can be won.

Step 3: Wait for the mistakes. The goal of all advocacy is to force our opponents' mistakes, which gives us the ability to shame our opponents and force them to either do what we want or lose more power.

Step 4: Make the mistakes the issue. If your opponent is ashamed or sorry, he will adopt your proposals or negotiate in good faith. If not, repeat steps 1 to 3 to force more mistakes and gain more leverage.

Step 5: Don't let go. Persistence often turns up the key lead, connection, or exposure that tips the campaign your way; keep your teeth in their tail until they agree to your terms.

Every successful campaign for change that I have been involved in or witnessed has boiled down to these basic steps. President Obama's failure during his first year as president to lead a genuine populist movement for change is directly the result of his failure to follow this formula. I can count on two hands the elected officials in Washington, D.C., today who practice this art regularly. A lot of politicians' efforts are geared toward credit and cameras, not creating the friction in the political establishments that's necessary to catalyze change. In the near future, though, the fate of presidents, politicians, and parties will depend on whether they listen to the public when it speaks. The fate of change will depend upon how the public voices its opinion.

Our opponents, as well as many of our allies, typically underestimate the great leveling force of public opinion. But change makers win by seizing upon popular opinion and forcing a confrontation with their opponents' views from the high ground of populist values. If President Obama had stood on the high ground of these values in his first year and confronted members of his own party who stood in the way of change, his public standing would be greater, and more progressive reform proposals would already be laws. The next generation of progressive leaders, or a reborn Obama, will have to learn from such mistakes. The public will not have its thirst for change quenched until such confrontations occur.

But how does an outsider know the opportunities for real change on the inside so she can seize them? How does an outsider create a record of progress on his or her issue—an essential aspect to moving that issue forward—if insiders don't want to listen? When and where is the best opportunity to catalyze change from the outside?

CHAPTER TWO

TEN RULES OF POPULIST POWER

Turning the tables on a powerful opponent revolves around a few core principles. By understanding what works and what hasn't for change makers, an informed public can better stake its claim to change. In fact, there are ten simple rules that can help an awakened public see and seize the outside opportunities for creating changes that the vast majority of Americans believe in.

Rule 1: Forcing Opponents to Make Mistakes Is the Goal of Effective Advocacy for Change; Promoting Issues Is Not Enough

Any major change in public policy requires a shift in the balance of power. A big opponent with a self-interest in the status quo stands in the way of the popularly sought reform, or that reform would have happened already. When the powerful opponents of change make egregious mistakes, they vastly amplify the value and force of our campaigns by proving the point we cannot demonstrate on our own: our opponents' values are out of touch with the public's.

Every campaign for real change must (1) define an opponent; (2) be waged to trip up the opponent; and (3) be ready to create change from the opponent's mistakes.

Consider how Congress finally banned so-called drive-through deliveries when HMOs tried to save some money by discharging newborns and their mothers from the hospital as early as eight hours after birth. The practice caught Congress's eye only after a Kaiser HMO bureaucrat got a little too cute in a memo written to staff at the HMO's flagship Sunset Boulevard hospital in Los Angeles. A whistleblower gave me the memo, titled "Positive Thoughts Regarding the Eight Hour Discharge." Among the "reasons" given for hospital staff to explain the hasty departure to new moms were "hospital food is not tasty" and "better bonding with siblings at home." Our exposure of the memo to the media became big news and was soon the subject of congressional hearings. Not only were the HMOs slighting motherhood, but data showed that newborns discharged early were twice as likely to end up in the emergency room with problems that proved to be expensive.

HMO executives were confronted with their penny-wise, pound-foolish policy. The rare glimpse into the cynical attitude of an HMO administration, coupled with exposures about mothers thrown out of the hospital before they learned to breast-feed, drove a Newt Gingrich–controlled Congress to require that newborns and their mothers not be discharged from the hospital any sooner than forty-eight hours without their consent. Congress rarely acts quickly, but when it does it's because there is little doubt what the public wants and that those who oppose the public's interest, like HMOs, cannot be trusted because they are so out of step. Only our opponents' mistakes can demonstrate so clearly why things need to change.

When opponents of new financial privacy protections claimed our privacy was not at risk, I proved the point in a novel way. I bought the Social Security numbers of Attorney General John Ashcroft, Defense Secretary Donald Rumsfeld, and other cabinet officials on the Internet for $26. When California legislation to protect financial privacy stalled in the statehouse, I decided to up the ante. I easily and legally bought the Social Security numbers of all the state legislators who opposed the legislation or refused to vote on it. Then I put up their partial Social Security numbers on the Internet along with the partial Social Security number of Governor Gray Davis. The politicians went ballistic. They called on the California Highway Patrol and attorney general to investigate and prosecute me. Their hot reaction to a risk to their personal privacy proved my point. It allowed me to turn the media spotlight they created onto their own failure to be concerned about the privacy of the public at large. The legislators drew attention to their own hypocrisy. Later that year, the California financial privacy protection legislation was revived, passed by the legislature and signed into law by Governor Davis.

True change almost always involves a public opinion war with those who control the status quo. This is where President Obama fell down on the job as a health reform change maker. He buckled early on to the drug companies, health insurers, and other medical complex lobbyists, as well as stalwarts in his party, rather than putting them to the test of whether their values were in sync with the public's. He didn't think he could fight the barrage of advertising the lobbies could afford to shape public opinion, and in doing that he put too little faith in the public and his own ability to use his opponents' own weight against them. Obama largely refused to put the opponents of real change in the Capitol and on K Street on the spot so that their mistakes would betray their interest in the status quo. Ironically, his success in finally enacting federal health insurance reforms was a result of one health insurance company's big mistake. When health reform looked like it was in the mortuary, Anthem Blue Cross raised premiums by 39 percent in California. President Obama had the good sense to seize on the public outrage and make the company a poster child for reform. The president effectively used his media pulpit to vector the public anger into a final, successful push for enactment of a new law, even though it had no teeth to stop premium increases like Anthem Blue Cross's. Obama's early capitulations to the medical insurance establishment had created a patient protection act that protected the medical industries' greatest interests and put new financial burdens on most Americans.

Public success often hinges on the quality of opponents' mistakes and the ability of change makers to exploit them. When opponents make mistakes that show they are out of touch, they amplify our case and weaken their own. Mistakes are the turning points of most populist battles, because mistakes provide the leverage and ammunition to finish the fight.

Rule 2: To Make Big Changes, Target the Little Things and a Few People

We have only so much energy, time, and capital to spend creating the changes we want. Often the impulse to get involved can be overwhelmed by how difficult it seems to change anything or anyone, particularly powerful institutions, industries, or officials. So it should be a comfort to know this trade secret of change makers: big changes are created by a small number of people who do little things right.

Think Paul Revere. In his bestseller *The Tipping Point*, Malcolm Gladwell shows how Revere had the right connections to knock on the right revolutionary leaders' doors, those who knew him, with his "sticky" message: "The British are coming!" Stickiness means that a message has an impact and is memorable. Another messenger who rode out in the opposite direction failed in the same charge because he wasn't as well connected as Revere, or apparently as persuasive. *The Tipping Point*, a must-read for effective advocates, sums up a growing body of research that shows how big changes on social issues come down to a few decisions and a few key decision makers. Whether you're trying to stem the tide of teen smoking, reduce your local crime rates, or sway opinion on any other issue, you need to influence the few to affect the many. Focus on identifying the smallest number of people who have the right connections and who can act with the greatest impact.

The small resources of my consumer group have necessitated that we find the right pressure points—the little things and right people—that will have a big impact. For proof that little things matter, consider the case of what happened after my colleagues and I took Arnold Schwarzenegger's red carpet away.

After his election as governor during the 2003 California recall, Arnold Schwarzenegger got an even bigger ego. The Republican governor embraced a thoroughly reactionary agenda. Although he had run for office as the anti-politician in a progressive state, Schwarzenegger called students, teachers, firefighters, and even the disabled "special interest groups" in an attempt to cut their budgets and pensions. But Schwarzenegger claimed that the label did not apply to big corporations that funded his campaign committee with tens of millions of dollars.

Shades of the same arrogance had surfaced during the recall, which is why my colleagues and I created "ArnoldWatch.org" to publicly track the hidden hand of special interests in the Schwarzenegger administration. We knew the California public would not look fondly upon being been lied to. Ultimately Governor Schwarzenegger was forced to apologize for his tactics. Chapter 6 offers the blow-by-blow of that campaign, but a key turning point hinged on doing a small thing right. Early on, a small group of us began in-your-face protests, starting at the governor's house on Super Bowl Sunday, and shadowing him across the state. Ultimately the protests grew to ten thousand strong. We knew that for a celebrity, used to basking in the public's spotlight, facing angry fans would be debilitating. The psychological turning point in the campaign came midway, during a premier for the Danny DeVito film *Be Cool* in Sacramento. DeVito was Schwarzenegger's acting partner in the movie *Twins* and a close friend.

We knew that if we could keep Schwarzenegger from walking the red carpet into that premier it would be symbolically devastating. The mighty California Nurses Association, great progressive allies, rented the Greek restaurant next door to the theatre, a block from the Capitol. Hundreds of nurses occupied the restaurant and its adjoining space on the red carpet with anti-Arnold signs and critical props. Schwarzenegger had to enter the theatre from the back exit. The symbolism said we would turn Arnold's celebrity around on him and that he couldn't show his face in California if he continued on his course. The governor suffered a near-knockout blow at the ballot box eight months later, when all five of the regressive ballot measures he opened fire with post-election were defeated. Schwarzenegger apologized the day after, reversed course, and regained some of his celebrity.

In a populist fight, targeting the right person can change the entire campaign. That's how Consumer Watchdog ended one insurance company CEO's two-decade war against voter-backed insurance regulation and won an end to insurers' redlining of poor and urban neighborhoods.

George Joseph is one of the four hundred richest men in the United States. He made his wealth from his Los Angeles–based company, Mercury Insurance. No one has more hatred for the insurance-regulating Proposition 103, nor has anyone done more to undo it. Joseph's company gave millions in campaign contributions to statehouse politicians to undermine the law. When Democrats bucked him, Joseph gave an even bigger, six-figure contribution to the opposite party. That sent a chilly message to both parties' leaders.

By the time Joseph turned eighty-four in 2006, California Insurance Commissioner John Garamendi had at long last finalized rules to end auto insurance rates based on motorists' zip codes. It was the last unfulfilled promise of the 1988 insurance reform initiative.

Mercury did a lot of business in urban areas, and George Joseph apparently didn't want to be told that he had to charge people based on how they drive, not where they live. So good drivers in the inner city were being required by the state to buy auto insurance, but insurers would not sell them a policy at an affordable price. In the poorest areas, the cheapest, most basic auto policies cost thousands of dollars a year because insurers didn't want to sell insurance there. So when the end to zip-code-based insurance was at hand, as final regulations were about to be implemented to make this change real, Joseph gave some top political consultants a big check and a green light to file a ballot measure overturning this long-awaited provision of Prop 103. After almost two decades of resistance, Joseph decided on all-out war.

Our response? We proposed a ballot measure of our own that would strictly curb Mercury's profits. We started a boycott of Mercury Insurance. But the key to turning George Joseph around was an Internet video we made about him for the "Boycott Mercury" Web site. Robert Greenwald, a friend and the progressive movie director behind *Iraq for Sale*, *Outfoxed*, and *Wal-Mart Movie*, sent a film crew to shadow the octogenarian from his luxurious Hancock Park home to his office. The camera crew confronted Joseph about the initiative in his office garage. They asked why Mercury would want to charge African Americans who lived in low-income communities and poorer zip codes more money. An angry letter from civil rights leaders also appeared on his desk. Within about a week, Mercury had withdrawn the initiative. But not before calling my colleague and Prop 103 author Harvey Rosenfield.

Joseph told Harvey his wife had asked him why there had been a video camera at his home. When he explained, she said she also thought it was wrong for his company to charge customers based on their zip code. A few months later, Joseph resigned as Mercury's CEO, though he retained his position as chairman of the board. New rules charging people based on how they drive, not where they live, finally took effect in 2008. California is the only state in the nation that forces insurers to base premiums on motorists' driving record, how far they drive, and how many years of experience they have, and not on where they live.

Only a few people were involved; only a small number of actions were needed. Less yielded more—something that is often not the case with staging a mass demonstration or other Herculean labor of protest. For example, for almost a year a group of doctors called "Physicians Who Care" worked to organize massive protests against HMO medicine on "Rescue Healthcare Day." The lead doctor bothered me nearly daily, and I kept warning him that the key to rescuing health care was what would happen the day after the protest. Nonetheless he continued to believe the outburst of physician energy would change everything. Of course, things didn't change on their own the day after the protests. The doctor and his group quickly disappeared. I didn't hear from him again for almost seven years. Just before the 2008 election he e-mailed to ask how he could raise questions about Senator McCain's failure to disclose his health records. I pointed him to Robert Greenwald, who had already created a video on the topic and a petition signed by thousands of doctors calling for a release of those records. Greenwald started out with only a few doctors but ultimately grew the effort to include thousands, a popular online video, and a front-page *New York Times* story that turned McCain's health into a campaign issue.

The question progressives must ask themselves is which small things and few people to target to turn things around.

Applying this to a national scale leads to some interesting options. Obama may not be the leader of the progressive movement, but it doesn't mean the movement cannot make him move. And if you were going to target a few people for the greatest change, you probably wouldn't have to look far. Progressives could demand a shake-up at the White House to oust Chief of Staff Rahm Emanuel. The jobs of Tim Geithner and Larry Summers should also be on the chopping block. The strategy of these three men is largely responsible for the setbacks for progressives in health care, financial regulation, and climate change legislation.

Rule 3: Simple Moral Sentiments Can Change the World When Public Opinion Propels Them

The public's power to create change against the wishes of powerful interest groups springs from simply phrased, widely shared moral sentiments. A short, simple articulation of the moral viewpoint driving a campaign sums up exactly what we are fighting for or against. The right sentence can rouse public opinion and spread the spirit of change like wildfire.

Here are some of the morals-based phrases that I have put to work:

- Newborns and their mothers should not be kicked out of the hospital eight hours after birth.
- Doctors, not HMO bureaucrats, should make medical decisions.
- Motorists should not be forced to choose between paying for auto insurance and buying food for their family.
- Oil companies should not be able to make more profit by making less gasoline.
- Our private financial information should not be bought and sold like pork bellies to the highest bidder.
- Insurance premiums should be based on how we drive, not where we live.

I have run successful campaigns around each of these irrefutable moral sentiments precisely because big industries and their allies in government tried to refute them. Campaigns for change rely on a social, ethical, or populist belief so powerful that our smartest opponents will not openly take issue with it for fear of losing their standing with the public. Most opponents do argue, though, and that is often their big mistake.

The sentiment of any issue-based campaign should (1) articulate a popular moral principle; (2) be simple and human; (3) put our opponents on the spot and force their tactical decision to support it or oppose it. Clever opponents will claim we are mistaken and that they don't really disagree with the populist sentiment and don't violate it. Then we must gather evidence to expose them to win our campaign, which creates opportunities for those with that information to come forward. Smart campaigners will have the evidence in their pocket first, ready to release once their opponent claims to support the sentiment.

The Kaiser bureaucrats who gave new meaning to the term "maternity leave" showed disregard for social mores about how to treat mothers and reaped their own shame. I spent years, with the help of whistleblowers, proving that HMO bureaucrats did indeed make medical decisions. HMOs tried to argue back with reasons why doctors should be paid bonuses to deny care to patients. They tried to defend their use of accounting manuals to dictate hospital stays and their bureaucrats in far-off states overriding a treating doctor's decisions. They found out quickly that offending the public's sensibilities is quicksand for those who want to maintain the status quo.

Campaigns for change, ironically, are often about preserving traditional values like fairness, justice, and privacy. They are about getting back something that has been lost. That is a powerful message that doesn't frighten the public: it involves returning lost values through new plans, not embarking on a dangerous new course. People fear change, even as they desire it. Popular change almost always is built on the bedrock of existing values that are threatened.

The greatest tactical objective of change makers is to expose our opponents' opposition to social mores, ethical customs, and the rule of law. Then we seize the moment to reassert these mores through new laws, stronger codes of conduct, or new decisions. The public should recognize these telltale signs and lend their opinion.

When you hear a moral sentiment worth fighting for, go for it. If you are trying to build a campaign, craft a statement that defines it. Moral sentiments have the power to create change when fueled by the last credible source of information in a culture of disintegrating trust: word of mouth. And Americans now have the best conductor of "word of mouth" in human history, the Internet.

Candidates already know how to win elections based on clearly expressed moral sentiments. Here are some of the ones that brought Obama to the White House:

- Health care should be accessible and affordable so that medical bills bankrupt no one.
- Americans must end dependence on the petroleum economy and stop gasoline prices from destroying our economy.
- Lobbyists and special interest groups shouldn't control Washington, D.C.

Republican senator Scott Brown, who foiled many of Obama's ambitions on the president's one-year anniversary in office, was remembered for this sentiment during the campaign: "This isn't Ted Kennedy's seat. It's the people's seat."

During campaigns, candidates have opponents to hold them accountable for such sentiments, but, after elections, too many interest groups are afraid to hold officials to their campaign pledges for fear of losing access. There's no more fertile ground for outsiders who seek to hold elected officials accountable to a platform of change than the field of the candidates' own words on the campaign trail. This was the tactic, for example, that finally forced Arnold Schwarzenegger to redefine special interests to include corporations that were giving him money. Even allies have to be reminded of the sentiments they espouse in order to keep them to reasonable time-lines for taking action. One moral sentiment Americans agree with is politicians shouldn't forget their promises after taking office.

Rule 4: Forget Sun Tzu: The Bigger the Fight, the Better the Odds; Fight Even If You Cannot Win Today, and Someday You'll Win without a Fight

Politics may be the art of the possible, but often "realism" or, as Hillary Clinton put it, "reality-based politics" undermines the possibility of genuine political change based on an outside game. By "outside game," I mean the notion that forces outside the Washington Beltway can move the insiders, based on the power of public opinion. Politicians tend not to believe or put much hope in the outside game unless the public's sentiment is a clear and present danger for them. Rousing public opinion begins with a strategy to invite conflict.

Sun Tzu's *The Art of War* is the classic strategy manual for poli-tics, business, and military conflict. The Chinese general argues that if your forces are unequal to your opponent's, you should avoid conflict. That may be true for classical warfare, but in the game of populist change, be it a fight with a government agency or a Fortune 500 company, the odds are always unequal. Engaging a fight with a more powerful opponent on an issue that may not seem winnable at the moment is essential because confrontation creates opportunities for your opponent to make mistakes and creates a public record of the battle. Look for the big fight if you want the big payoff, even if you lose some battles.

When our consumer group first took on the HMOs' cost-cutting practices, many of our allies said they were too strong and we would alienate a potential force for universal health care by trying to bring them under control. But we changed their worst abuses by exposing and confronting them.

When he went to the California ballot with insurance reform

Prop 103 in 1988, Harvey Rosenfield had to deal with angering allies who claimed he could never beat the property-insurance industry's money. Consumer groups and trial lawyers wanted to avert a ballot war and cut a deal with insurance companies, who ultimately put their own anti-consumer agenda on the ballot to confuse voters. Harvey wouldn't back down, even though he had raised no significant money to spend on a campaign. Insurers spent over $60 million against Harvey's landmark ballot measure and on making the case for their own, and that turned out to be their downfall. The companies so saturated the airwaves with television advertisements against Prop 103 that the public realized insurers were against the measure. That convinced 51 percent of voters to support the ballot measure, because it was the real-deal insurance reform. You have to love populist jujitsu.

When matched against a much more powerful opponent, the more our opponent attacks, the stronger we become. So provoke the more powerful opponent to attack. The more a powerful opponent engages and acknowledges us, the more power our arguments gain in the court of public opinion. When the more powerful opponent lends us his spotlight, he places us on the same stage and credentials our point of view. The powerful attack only when threatened. The more we attack, the more they react, and the stronger we become.

Rule 5: Creating the Record Creates the Seeds of Change

Building a record of one's battles and one's opponents' errors is critical to the power of the less-resourced advocate. Letters, demands, exchanges, and exposés that confront opponents—and force them to respond publicly—create a record that can later be used against your target. In the court of public opinion, creating a public record and forcing a decision maker to respond is the equivalent of the legal discovery process in the court of law. You are trying to uncover a discrepancy and take advantage of a mistake, now or later.

A campaign that can and will create a record is a triple threat to a powerful opponent.

1. We can lose the battle and still negatively affect our opponent's standing in the court of public opinion.
2. We can lose the battle yet create the conditions by which we can win the war.
3. We can win the battle by forcing our opponent to make a big mistake.

Building a record builds our power and leverage because an opponent who knows of our ability to build the record and willingness to wait for the right moment to use it will have to take us seriously.

Consider the most famous example of a well-fought loss that led to victory. The debates between Abraham Lincoln and Stephen Douglas as they vied to become the U.S. senator from Illinois are among the most famous in American history. Lincoln lost the election, but the record he established in those debates won him the platform to ascend to the presidency a few years later.

Or consider a more recent case from my consumer group's files, one that shows the value of building a public record on an opponent.

As recently as 2005, then Senate majority leader Bill Frist of Tennessee was a presumed front-runner for the GOP presidential nomination to succeed President Bush. Today he's not even in the Senate. Here's the story.

When Frist controlled the U.S. Senate in 2003 and 2004 as majority leader, he made a big mistake. At the time there was little chance that he or the Senate Ethics Committee would respond favorably to my consumer group's written concerns about his conflicts of interest with his family's business. But we created a record that years later undermined Frist's power and helped to end his political career.

Frist, a doctor whose family controlled one of the nation's largest hospital chains, was then backing a Senate bill to limit legal accountability for doctors and hospitals when they commit medical malpractice. We publicly demanded that Frist sell at least $25 million of stock he held in the Frist family company, HCA. HCA was one of America's largest hospital companies and owner of HCI, the nation's fifth biggest medical malpractice insurer. No one had ever heard of this issue before we put it on the map for the media and opinion leaders, but afterward it was closely tracked.

"HCI, HCA and your entire family stand to profit directly from the passage of malpractice caps legislation," we wrote to Frist. Of course, Frist did not divest his stock, nor recuse himself from the medical malpractice vote. We got some press at the time, but, more importantly, the record we created came back to haunt Senator Frist two years later.

When Frist finally sold the stock in September 2005, he did it just before the stock price tumbled, suggesting his family had given him an insider tip. A lot of eyes were watching by then. Frist was subpoenaed by the Justice Department and the SEC in an insider trading investigation of his well-timed sale. The investigation was made public two days after we sent another letter calling for an inquiry to the SEC and U.S. attorney. The record we had created years before, when it looked like we could not win the fight, was significant in the demise of Frist's political career.

The scandal put an end to Frist's presidential ambitions. His medical malpractice legislation, stained by the insider-trading allegation, never passed. The record, not the outcome of the initial battle, mattered most in the end.

Doing the right thing at the right time usually produces the right result in the end. The tension between progressives, who want their officials to stand on principle, and politicians, who want accomplishments before the next election, is constant and inevitable. It's our job to urge the politicians to put what's right over what's convenient.

Rule 6: Keep It Human, Put People First

Never underestimate the power of one person's story to change the world; indeed such stories may be the only thing that ever has. The sincere experiences of individuals who have suffered injustice are the best weapons against injustice. Winning campaigns are about the triumph of fundamental human truth, so real people with genuine stories are the best messengers of populist campaigns.

The language of the status quo is often statistical, actuarial, and data-based. This is not to say proponents of change don't have science and statistics on their side. It's just that opponents of change often base their objections on the hard, cold numbers that only accountants can muster and manipulate to show how they will bust budgets, bankrupt businesses, and break up families. My favorite example is tobacco companies' argument against the Czech government's smoking cessation plan. The industry's actuarial study found that the country's health care costs would skyrocket since people would live longer.

While it's tempting to mix it up with scientists when you know you're right, change-making campaigns typically mobilize the public and affect politics by sticking to the human case. Consider the medical patients' wars in Washington, D.C., the classic arena where critical public policy battles with significant human consequences are too often fought over statistics and computer models. Powerful opponents use selective data to defuse change. So in the mid-1990s I pioneered a method to make sure Washington politicians looked patients in the eye before they took away their legal rights.

Lawmakers on Capitol Hill were engaged in a debate over whether victims of medical negligence should have limits on their rights to go to court and recover damages for malfeasance. Of course, the medical-insurance industry instigated that discussion. So we began our first "casualty of the day" campaign. In the pre-Internet world, fax machines were the cutting edge of communication. Every day for five months, every congressional representative, every senator, and key members of the press received a fax with a picture and tragic story of a casualty of medical malpractice who needed his or her rights preserved. I knew the campaign was successful when the medical-insurance lobby's public relations machine answered back with its own "medical miracle of the moment," highlighting life-saving medical advances. As I commented at the time, the industry's reaction was like Ford putting out a press release about every Pinto gas tank that didn't explode.

The power of the campaign was in its cumulative impact. Every day, another story. Legislative staff and the media paid attention. The drumbeat built. We defended against the assault on injured patients' legal remedies.

A few years later, the time came to go on the offensive for the legal rights of HMO patients. We warmed up the fax machine again. The HMOs spent millions on television advertising to stop us. Here's how CNN's Brooks Jackson described the "HMO casualty of the day" campaign at the time: "The industry has its advertising too, but far more effective is this shoestring consumer group. A fax a day to keep the HMOs at bay." The patients-first tactic fueled landmark HMO patients'-rights reforms throughout the nation.

More recently, I saw the "people-first" principle work when one woman with a compelling story was able to fell a whole industry. It's the case of "Dana vs. Goliath."

With health insurance costs skyrocketing in 2006, insurers hatched a plan to remove themselves from the patients'-rights laws that were passed in forty-four states in the late 1990s and early 2000s. The industry explained that the insurance companies wanted to "reduce their costs of compliance" so insurance would be cheaper. It sounded simple enough to President Bush and Congress, who were about to enact the plan. Attorneys general, governors, and state insurance commissioners complained, but it looked like the industry had the votes.

Then Dana Christensen came to Capitol Hill with my Consumer Watchdog colleagues Carmen Balber and Jerry Flanagan.

Christensen had been working with my consumer group to warn against the very type of "junk health insurance" policy that we feared would become the norm if state regulation were bypassed. She and her husband, Doug, had been technically insured, yet Dana was left with $450,000 in unpaid medical bills when her husband died of bone cancer.

The fine print in her insurance policy had no limit on "out-of-pocket cost." So she had to pay most of the costs of his chemotherapy and cancer care. On his deathbed, Doug asked Dana to divorce him so she would not have to be liable for the medical bills. She refused. In the end, only because of a lawsuit under state law, which prevented fraudulent representations, was Dana able to recoup the cost of those bills from the insurer.

Dana flew into Washington on Monday, on the heels of a PBS *NOW* news story about her case that aired the previous Friday. She held a press conference with Senators Edward Kennedy and Richard Durbin, then lobbied other senators. The power of her story stopped the legislation dead in its tracks.

"What's the point of paying for health insurance and then, when you need it, discovering the benefits you thought were promised and paid for just aren't there?" Dana asked. "That's what happened to my husband Doug and me."

Human truth is very hard for a human being, even the most hardened Washington politician, to turn away from.

Rule 7: Make It Personal for Decision Makers

Confrontation creates change in human beings. It forces them to evaluate their positions because it warns of the consequences if they do not. If you want recalcitrant decision makers to change their ways, confront them personally and publicly about their actions. Don't just tell them why they are wrong; show them how their position reflects on their personal character.

Publicly confront them in a way that forces them to examine their person, not merely their positions. Then they must take inventory of what you have described and stand by it or change it. Successful decision makers typically change to conform with deep-seated social mores and ethical customs. Sometimes they even become your allies. Less-successful opponents compound their mistakes and dig themselves in deeper, which can give us more leverage over them. Making it personal means not name-calling or making spurious allegations, but forcing a confrontation with an opponent on the battlefield of values.

When he was in the California Legislature, Gray Davis, who

later lost a recall election as governor in 2003, sponsored legislation to put the faces of missing children on milk cartons. When my consumer group wanted to force Davis, as governor, to sign a strong HMO patient protection law in 1998, Harvey Rosenfield came up with the idea of putting the governor's face on faux milk cartons. "Missing: California Governor. Last Seen at Fundraiser with HMO Executives." We printed up thousands of the cartons and delivered them to hotel rooms in the San Francisco Hilton the night before Davis was scheduled to give a big breakfast speech. The flyer had all the details about how Davis met behind closed doors with HMO executives, raised big campaign contributions from them, and said he would not sign the tough patient protection law we wanted.

Davis received a chilly reception at the breakfast speech. He was upset by our tactics, especially a letter about the issue that we had Ralph Nader send to him, and went into a *San Francisco Chronicle* editorial meeting with a chip on his shoulder and angry that, as the governor, he was being taken to task. At that editorial board meeting he was asked about the patients' rights legislation and made his big mistake. He said of the legislature, "Their job is to implement my vision." When those words appeared in the newspaper, he was forced to retreat. The legislature put a very tough piece of legislation on his desk and he signed it. After the HMO patients' bill of rights signing ceremony, Davis stopped me as I was walking in a crosswalk. He leaned out of the backseat of his Lincoln town car and said, "Jamie, you have to give me high marks for this one. I want to see it on the front page." Never underestimate politicians' regard for their self-image.

Making it personal obviously often comes with a personal cost. The governor was very angry with us for a long time. We heard from donors that Governor Davis had personally called them and asked that they not contribute to our group. I knew one of the organizers of that Gray Davis breakfast very well. He wouldn't talk to me for years. I have no doubt, though, that had we not personalized the issues, Davis would have carried through on his threat to veto the stronger patient protections.

Rule 8: Seize the Moment—Don't Pick Your Time, Have the Goods and Let Your Time Pick You

Timing is the fulcrum of populist power. We cannot always choose it but we have to be ready for it to choose us. Create the record, plan for the right moments, and windows of opportunity should open to our advantage. These rare openings are awakenings in a public consciousness about an issue that can trump the human tendency to fear transitions and change itself. Moments of opportunity, events that focus public opinion like a beam, must be seized or they are lost. If it seems like the right time to jump into a campaign, don't wait.

For example, the collapse of Enron following the burst of the dot-com stock bubble left people wondering what had happened not only to their nest eggs, but also to corporate governance rules. Our consumer group knew it provided a moment to act.

In the 1980s, an industrial accident led to a new California law requiring that managers tell regulators about workplace hazards or go to jail. We wanted the same individual accountability for corporate executives on financial matters. Our first stab at reform was California legislation requiring that executives report financial fraud to government authorities or face jail time. We also wanted to create new protections for whistleblowers and a 1-800 hotline for them to report problems. Big business targeted the bill for defeat, calling it "tattletale" legislation and claiming the disloyal should not have new rights.

In the end, the legislature and the governor bowed to popular opinion and granted whistleblowers their protections. They wouldn't, however, make individual corporate executives personally liable for their financial statements. It took the U.S. Congress to do that a little later, seizing on the idea under the Sarbanes-Oxley Act.

Corporate executives today must personally sign their financial statements and are personally accountable for the veracity. There is not a single provision of Sarbanes-Oxley that CEOs complain about more, which makes us happy and shareholders a little more secure.

Or consider the case of our "Rx Express." The 2004 presidential election provided a moment of clarity for many Americans about the high cost of prescription drugs. The issue infected the presidential debate between President George W. Bush and Senator John Kerry. So our consumer group chartered two private trains—dubbed the Rx Express—to take seniors to Canada to buy cheaper drugs, right in the middle of the presidential debates. My colleague Jerry Flanagan wanted to show how Americans pay about 60 percent more for prescription drugs than the people of other nations. The next president would then have to lower prescription drug costs.

One train went up the West Coast, another up the East Coast, picking up seniors along the way while we held whistle-stop press conferences in their communities. A train began in Florida and stopped for passengers and press conferences all the way to Toronto. The other train did the same from San Diego to Vancouver. In Canada, the Rx Express riders saved an average of 60 percent off the prescription drug prices they paid in the United States for a total annual savings of $2,000 each. And the journeys made a big impression, in the media and with the presidential candidates.

The Rx Express train trips generated more than three hundred television appearances, with a Nielsen audience of sixty-five million, sixty newspaper articles, and one hundred radio interviews. The provision of prescription drug benefits to seniors became a central issue in the election and ultimately translated to an expansion of Medicare, albeit a faulty one that will be corrected at the right moment.

We had one amazing windfall of luck during the trip, when the Bush administration tried to intimidate our seniors. Government officials boarded the eastern-seaboard train at its last stop before the Canadian border looking for drugs. On the night of a presidential debate no less. Of course, that mistake only gave Jerry and his crew of seniors another round of media stories. The only error we made was not asking then state senator Barack Obama to come along. Had we, he may not have been able to retreat in 2009 from his campaign pledge to reduce the nation's prescription drug bill through bulk purchasing.

Rule 9: Exploit a Powerful Opponent's Fear of Falling to Achieve Victory without Combat

Our powerful opponents, if they're smart, will always be more afraid of us than we are of them. We have far less to lose. I had that revelation early in my career as a public advocate. At the time, I worked as an advocate for the homeless and was vacationing with my wife on the Yucatán Peninsula near the Mayan ruins of Chichen Itza. As I ascended the great pyramid, the congressional welfare reform fight was on my mind—in particular how to fight on behalf of people most others in America didn't care about. At the homeless shelter where I worked, there were several children. Their mothers did not have child care, so they couldn't hold jobs and keep a roof over their children's heads. But Congress wanted to take away their aid without providing them the child care they needed to go to work.

I remember how the climb up the narrow steps was hard and the view of the surrounding jungle was magnificent. But what really stuck with me was the feeling of standing at the top, on the broad plateau looking out on the dense forests of the Yucatán. My knees went weak. There was plenty of space to stand, yet as I looked toward the edge, I could not help fearing that I would fall, as improbable as I knew it was. It occurred to me then that this is how those at the top of any pyramid of power must feel—fearful of the fall, worried about their knees being cut out from under them, ever conscious of the ineluctable force of gravity pulling them down. It spurred me on to more aggressive tactics to get elected officials to pay attention to the families in our shelter.

I have taken that lesson with me. Exploiting our opponents' fear of their own missteps, of falling from their perch, is the quickest way to win. Show them how bad they look early on in order to have them change course or preempt an attack. It's a lesson some colleagues and I recently put into practice against the leaders of Yahoo and Intel to stop an assault on class action lawsuits in California.

In 2007, Intel was a household brand with tremendous popular approval. That's probably why the company was called on to chair a corporate consortium in California bent on eliminating consumer class action lawsuits. The consortium chose Intel—rather than one of its drug companies, tobacco makers, or insurers—to occupy the top spot as it filed a ballot measure to put up so many legal hurdles that ripped-off consumers would never have been able to file class action cases holding the responsible corporation accountable. Before signatures were even collected to place the initiative on the ballot, though, a group of us trying to stop the effort caught a huge break.

I heard on National Public Radio that Intel was in the middle of a flap over an insensitive advertisement that many considered racist. The print ad, which had been published overseas, featured a white manager standing over six African-American sprinters kneeling before him. The ad proclaimed, "Maximize Your Power." Intel withdrew the advertisement and apologized. Still, I knew immediately that Intel had made the fatal mistake that could be used to force withdrawal of the initiative. Its brand was now vulnerable. A major purpose behind class action lawsuits is to protect the civil rights of Americans, and Intel had shown a callous disregard on matters of ethnic sensitivity.

During the next two weeks, my consumer group launched an Internet campaign that asked, "Is Intel racist inside?" We called on the company to withdraw both the advertisement and the initiative. After our e-activists sent thirty thousand faxes online to the board of directors and kicked up a lot of bad press, Intel and its corporate consortium announced that the initiative would not go forward. In an internal e-mail to the consortium's board of directors, a proponent blamed the retreat on the fact that the initiative campaign would be more "high profile" than initially anticipated.

"Fear of the fall" was directed not only at Intel, but at one of its key board members, Susan Decker. Decker had just taken the reins at Yahoo, right after CEO Terry Semel resigned for a major misstep. We knew Decker was particularly vulnerable to criticism as a new CEO. So a member of our group, Chris Lehane, who had been a lawyer and spokesperson in the Clinton White House, and Will Robinson of the New Media Firm created and produced a cable television ad that ran in Silicon Valley targeting Decker and providing her office phone number.

The ad opened with the Yahoo logo flashing on a white background while the announcer declared, "Yahoo is a leading global brand." Then a photo of Decker swept in next to the Yahoo logo and the announcer continued, "And as president, Susan Decker helps set Yahoo's vision." The Intel logo swooped in, too, and the announcer added, "But she's also on the board on Intel." At that point, an image of the controversial Intel advertisement slowly crept onto the screen. "And Intel had been using advertising that has been called offensive, even racist," said the announcer. Eventually, the image cut to a ballot box, and word *discrimination* with a big "no" circle over it. "Now," continued the announcer, "Intel is supporting a ballot measure that makes it tougher to fight discrimination, and harder to stop big corporations, HMOs, and oil companies from hurting consumers." At the ad's close, the Enron logo flew in and pushed out the word *discrimination*, then "HMO" pushed out "Enron" and then finally an oil derrick pushed out "HMO" and the image changed back to Susan, with her phone number plastered below. The voice-over concluded, "So call Susan, and tell her maybe it's time to start bringing Yahoo's vision to Intel."

The same week the advertisement aired, Intel decided to withdraw its ballot measure. Fear cuts both ways, of course. The public's fear of change is often the target of our opponents' campaigns to defeat reform. Special interest campaigns to stop popularly sought-after changes operate from a standard playbook that feeds upon the public's well-conditioned fears and seeks to distract from the public benefits of a reform. Seeing through the standard ploys, though, may make it easier to resist them. The following table shows six of the most common "fear points" that opponents of change use in both their political attacks to counter reform and the claims they frequently make. You may recognize how the GOP and the medical-insurance complex effectively used these arguments in the court of public opinion to fear-monger about the Democrats' health care reform plan during 2010. The Tea Party's playbook is little different,

Table 1. Common Fear Factors Invoked by Opponents of Change	
Fear Point	**Common Deceptions**
Big government	New bureaucracy: New inefficient bureaucracies, like death panels, will get between you and what you need to survive
	Unwanted invasion of privacy: Government will know what it is in your underwear drawer, publicize it, and make you buy a clean pair, even if you don't want it.
	Taxpayer cost: Your taxes will go through the roof and your kids will have to pay even more.
Loss of Choice	Whenever government gets involved, markets give you less freedom to choose. No more picking your doctor or access to the best medicines. And there'll be Soviet-style breadlines.
Rising Prices	Government advice always raises prices. Any change that regulates an industry will double the price that industry charges you, because all that red tape has a big price tag for compliance.
Unintended Consequences	The smallest points of proposals should be your worst fear because evil bureaucrats will seize on the fine print to do unimaginable things. That's what always happens when things change in a corrupt world.
Slippery Slope	If you make any change to help people, the next step is socialism. That's what Karl Marx advocated. Public options don't work because the next step is turning the USA into the USSR.
Job Killer	Businesses will shut down rather than comply and more jobs will flee across the border.

as it's been constructed by many longtime GOP operatives, like Dick Armey, looking for a more populist chorus.

Appeals to the public's fear that destroy reform efforts are typically strategic arson: a fire of fear sparked on the dry brush of parched populist ground. For example, the drug companies and insurers could ignite Americans' fear of the bureaucrats in President Clinton's health care plan because the Clintons failed to keep the populist soil fertile by engaging public opinion. Instead, the Clintons engaged in back-door negotiations with so-called stakeholders. President Obama fared far better with his health reform effort during the summer of 2009, when it contained a public health insurance option to compete with the private health insurance market, supported consistently by the vast majority of Americans in poll after poll. Obama lost ground to the fear factors only when he abandoned the public option and his progressive base. That's when support for his plan fell under the 50 percent mark. The best prevention against public fear destroying a populist campaign for change is to constantly nourish public opinion and stay true to your message and values.

Rule 10: Don't Worry about Your Seat at the Table; Find the Rock to Throw through the Window

The big coalition, the most famous names, or the politically diverse negotiating partners do not signal that the changes being espoused reflect a consensus about the public's opinion—or even have a chance of success. In fact, when insiders are all on the same page, it's very likely that their proposal won't shake things up at all. Shaking endangers their interests.

Consider one of the biggest illusions going in politics: the notion of "bipartisan" change. Bipartisanship has become the new Good Housekeeping seal of approval in America. Take the "bipartisan budget compromise"—the holy grail for state and federal politicians trying to escape for summer vacations as I write this. No one knows what's really in the compromise measure. No one cares because it carries the bipartisan brand, even though it's loaded with pork for both parties. Some think that in a deeply divided political system, anytime Republicans and Democrats can agree, it must be progress. How can a consensus among the traditional enemies of change reflect a real shift? Did they suddenly come to God? Too often, bipartisanship is simply code for the political class and the interest groups that finance them to gang up on the little guys.

Many public interest groups, like their counterparts in industries, scramble for a seat at the negotiating table, even though they don't have many chips to play in the game. The cost of that seat can often be the trading away of deeply held convictions—which are the only strength of populist campaigns. The seat at the table also robs them of the right to condemn the process itself, possibly the one chip they do have. On every issue our consumer group has worked on, there have always been groups anxious to take their picture with the governor or the president regardless of the integrity of the outcome. We have never wanted a seat at the table. That seat can compromise your position and the public's desires, and it also can take away your ability to force an opponent's mistake.

Consider Obamacare. To get the drug companies, doctors, and insurance companies on board, President Obama gave away the toughest reforms that would have energized the public and given him power to enact more progressive reform. Similarly, President Clinton had a clear electoral mandate to reform health care in 1992, but he squandered the opportunity when he invited all the health care "stakeholders" to the table to hash out the details in large rooms where a mediator oversaw dialogues about medical minutiae.

I was invited to the White House to talk health care reform during the Clinton years. To clear the security check, I needed to provide my Social Security number. A seat at the table didn't turn my proposals into law, but, years later, I received a letter from the National Archive warning that a White House laptop with my Social Security number on it was missing. My visit to the inside put me in danger of being a victim of identify theft.

The Clintons, when they tried their hand at health care reform during Bill Clinton's presidency, could not articulate a clear plan on a single piece of paper to the public. They saw their real strength, the public's high opinion of their efforts, shrink. Obama fared no better in Year One, similarly attempting to appease the medical-insurance establishment, rather than fighting them to reduce their charges and make health care more affordable. In the end, the Clintons lost the public when insurers and drug companies went to the "outside" and teamed up in a successful public relations effort that fanned the public's worst fears about government bureaucracy. Those infamous "Harry and Louise" television advertisements in 1993 featured a middle-aged couple voicing concerns about losing their choices under the Clinton plan and government bureaucrats interfering with their medical care. In 2008, a coalition of businesses, drug companies, hospitals, and other Washington advocacy groups, called "Health Care First," scored points with a riff on the Harry and Louise advertising. This time the couple talked about how "health care costs are up again, small companies are forced to cut their plans . . . and too many people are falling through the cracks. Whoever the next president is, health care should be at the top of his agenda. Bring everyone to the table and make it happen." The table, of course, did not produce the change Americans hungered for.

Pragmatically, here's a simple truth. Setting up an opponent for a fall after you have seen his children's pictures at the lunch table is always harder than being ruthless with a faceless rival. Every time I spoke on a panel with an HMO executive, for example, I felt an impulse to call her before I threw out my next salvo against her company, even though in the end I knew it would hurt my cause to deal with the problem quietly. After spending a little time with Governor Gray Davis, a genuinely nice guy, I felt pangs of guilt about his recall, even though I knew our public criticism of him was necessary during the California energy crisis.

Our opponents fear us more if we refuse to sit down at the table with them. The stone we can throw to shatter their glass house is more meaningful. It's harder to take aim at the house of someone you have come to consider a colleague.

An outsider can shift the entire debate away from consensus at a table dominated by insiders and toward what the public really wants and deserves. Being an outsider is not merely a tactical decision to muster power, but a philosophical choice of standing with those you represent, who are also on the "outside," and trying to turn the inside out through greater transparency, disclosure, and public decision making. Populist power resides in holding details up to public scrutiny and applying our social mores to them, since insiders tend to disregard widely held public attitudes in favor of political expediency.

The same rule usually applies to allies as well as enemies, since many of our allies eat with our enemies. Our general rule is: go at it alone, because the time lost in a coalition can cost you the opportunity for victory.

The role of outsider keeps us above the fray, more able to create the record we need and stay two moves ahead of where the game is being played at the moment.

Consider the case of how I became the only Californian in memory to be kicked out of a legislative hearing for mentioning campaign contributions.

The scene: the California senate insurance committee, May 2003. The senate majority leader, Don Perata, had accepted $25,000 from George Joseph's Mercury Insurance company. Then he authored legislation that would allow Mercury to surcharge previously uninsured motorists. Voters had approved a law specifically preventing such motorists from paying more, and the legislature wasn't allowed to change it. The state insurance commissioner wouldn't grant Mercury that right, either. So Mercury CEO Joseph went to Perata, a close ally of the senate insurance committee chair I sat across from that day.

I testified to the committee that if senators had not received so much in campaign contributions from Mercury, then the legislation would never have come before the committee, since it was illegal. If it did pass, I said, the courts would overturn it. The state would pay my consumer group's legal fees. That did not go over well. The chair warned me not to mention campaign contributions again. I continued, believing it was my right to speak freely. That's when the sergeant at arms took my microphone and removed me from the table.

I was aware, of course, that I was not winning votes on the committee. But reporters were listening. I wanted the record to reflect that the legislation was greased with insurer money and that the measure was illegal.

The *Los Angeles Times* reported my ejection the next day, and the reasons, and later editorialized against the legislation. My power came not from being at the table, but from being removed from it. The legislation favoring Mercury Insurance did ultimately pass and was signed into law. Our consumer group sued, and a court invalidated the law. The state paid our lawyer's fees. Senator Perata subsequently came under FBI investigation for pay-to-play scandals and spent more than $1.4 million defending himself. The head of Mercury Insurance received a subpoena through one of his other investment businesses.

The angry committee chair back then was California state senator Jackie Speier. Ironically, she went to Washington in 2008 as a congressional representative and, during a particularly frustrating fight, told one of my colleagues that the public interest groups in DC were "anemic." She suggested that Consumer Watchdog open an office in town. We took her advice in 2009 and have been practicing the art of outsider politics inside the Beltway ever since.

These ten "moves" add up to the ability of small, righteous populist campaigns to apply leverage to more powerful foes who stand in the way of change or are trying to worsen the lot of the public in some other way. Populist change making is an art, not a science. Like any art, it's an ordering activity: making the right move with appropriate pressure in a certain manner can throw the most powerful opponent off balance and lead to victory.

But there's no precise equation that yields the same result each time. That's why political scientists often cannot factor the populist equation into their analysis. Jujitsu relies on intuition and anticipation. The same catalysts don't always produce the same result. A lot more would change in this country if more Americans were aware of the essence of populist power and could anticipate and aid the moves they support. As chapter 3 shows, each of us with access to the Internet has at our disposal the most effective means ever to make our voice heard for social, economic, and political change.

CHAPTER THREE

ROUSING PUBLIC OPINION IN A NEW MEDIA AGE

The art of capturing the public's imagination and mobilizing popular opinion has changed radically in recent years. It used to be that my colleagues and I could expose an outrage on the front page, confront the troublemakers on radio and television, and force a mistake that editorial pages, columnists, and news anchors would sound off about. When the decision makers felt enough heat, they would decide to flee the kitchen, concede to public opinion, and accept change.

The shape of the media has altered dramatically. We can still make a politician change his tune after facing the music in the press, but it's harder and harder. Fewer people read newspapers. The number of journalists is rapidly declining, resulting in far less journalistic investigation. Hard-hitting television news journalism has largely been abandoned in favor of car chases, Hollywood train wrecks, and eye candy. Americans gather their information and entertainment from hundreds of cable television channels, a slew of satellite radio stations, and hundreds of thousands of Internet sites. The explosion of social media and online interaction and conversations has pulled us into yet newer circles of information exchange. More Americans visit Twitter every month than visit the *New York Times, Washington Post,* and *Wall Street Journal* sites combined. Monthly traffic on Facebook is larger than that all of the major newspapers in America combined. The public's attention is far more diffuse.

On the other hand, every individual has an unprecedented opportunity to shape the course of history from her own computer, simply by creatively exercising her opinions and judgment.

The Internet and social media have quickly and effectively propelled simple exposures, confrontations, and mistakes to create big changes that *New York Times* reports could not have achieved. The reason is that the Internet is an immediate reflection of public opinion without filters, translators, or amplifiers. And it's a multimedia effect—sound, camera, and action! A damaging newspaper exposé requires some interpretation about its political consequences and the "legs" it has with the public. Ten thousand e-mails into a Congressman's office in two hours, four hundred thousand signatures on an online petition, or one million views of a video are an immediate measure of the public's concern. An uploaded YouTube video, smoking-gun document, salient photo, or particularly "viral" e-mail message on the Internet can propel big changes overnight. The right tweet can assemble an angry mob to greet a politician in a matter of hours. Table 2 shows some of the differences between the old and new ways of spreading the word.

Change can be a stone's throw away on the Internet when it's the right stone artfully propelled at the right time and target. Following are just a few examples of how the Internet can be the most effective new slingshot for propelling American public opinion.

- The father of an American soldier who had returned from a fifteen-month tour of duty in Afghanistan's most dangerous terrain posted a YouTube video showing deplorable barracks conditions at Fort Bragg, North Carolina, where his son was stationed. Ed Frawley's narrated montage of still images showed broken ceiling

Table 2. Old Media vs. New Media

Traditional Media	Internet Media
Lecture	Discussion
More likely to be factually accurate	More likely to be socially salient
Limited range of voices favors decision makers' paradigms and points of view	Unlimited range of voices allows opportunities for insurgent voices and views
Biggest asset: manageable, credible, and authoritative	Biggest weakness: unmanageable, unaccountable, and non-authoritative
Biggest weakness: elitist and not reflective of popular sentiment	Biggest asset: immediately accountable and reflective of popular sentiment

tiles, mold, rust, peeling paint, broken sewer drains with sewage-gas leaks, busted toilets, and a soldier squatting in a sink trying to clear inches of overflowing sewage in the barracks bathrooms. The YouTube video, which made a vivid case that this is no way to treat heroes, provided ways to protest to officials and the media and provoked the army to quickly commit to repairs.

• The balance of power in the United States Senate shifted from Republican to Democrat on November 9, 2006, when incumbent Republican senator George Allen of Virginia lost his seat. His defeat was propelled by a racist remark captured on video at a campaign stop and spread over the Internet. Allen called a videotaping volunteer for his opponent— a college freshmen who happened to be of Indian descent—"macaca," slang for a type of monkey and a racial slur. Allen said on video, "This fellow over here . . . Macaca or whatever his name is, he's with my opponent. . . . Let's give a welcome to Macaca here, welcome to America and the real world of Virginia." Allen soon found himself in Tim Russert's hot seat on *Meet the Press*, claiming he didn't know what *macaca* meant and had made it up. The mistakes led to Democrat Jim Webb claiming victory and the fifty-first Senate seat for the Democratic party that election night.

• In quintessential Internet jujitsu, MIT graduate Jonah Peretti turned a gimmick on Nike's Web site, called "Personal ID," against the company's labor practices. Nike offered shoes with a personalized word or phrase near the company's trademark swoosh. Peretti chose the word *sweatshop*, and Nike made the mistake of refusing to send him his personalized shoes. The e-mail showing Nike's refusal was forwarded to an estimated 10 million people worldwide, caught the attention of the traditional media, and mobilized public opinion against Nike's sweatshop labor practices.

• MoveOn cofounder Joan Blades calls herself an "accidental activist. . . . We put together a one-sentence petition [against President Clinton's impeachment]. . . . We sent it to under a hundred of our friends and family, and within a week we had a hundred thousand people sign the petition. At that point, we thought it was going to be a flash campaign, that we would help everyone connect with leadership in all the ways we could figure out, and then get back to our regular lives. A half a million people ultimately signed and we somehow never got back to our regular lives." MoveOn, which now has over five million members, became one of the most successful Internet-based political groups in America, having influenced public opinion on elections, wars, and other issues. The group was the first to pioneer small-donor Internet political fund-raising, air political television commercials created by average people and voted on in contests by its members, and convene a virtual online primary to influence actual presidential primaries. MoveOn's e-mail list is much smaller than Obama's but has had a far bigger effect after the 2009 election.

• Comedian Steven Colbert received a chilly reception at the 2006 White House Correspondents' Association dinner when he gave a brilliant satire of President Bush, who sat a few seats away, of the White House press corps, and of official Washington and their dumbed-down version of politics, the war, and political coverage. Colbert said what so many Americans thought. As Colbert noted, only 30 percent of Americans supported Bush at the time. "It's not a half empty glass, it's two-thirds of the glass empty." The press coverage of the event largely ignored and dismissed the satire, including the network news. But the video caught fire on YouTube and the Internet. Colbert's riff on Bush's awful public opinion ratings, his staged photo opportunities, and the distortion of the truth in Washington spoke truth to power and rallied public opinion against the president's wartime propaganda and the press's deference to the White House. The Internet was the only platform where the public could see and spread this searing populist critique of official Washington from within its own walls. A video from a camera locked on President Bush during the event, showing his reaction to Colbert, garnered more YouTube views, 1.6 million, than Colbert's original material. Americans got to see Bush's facial reaction to popular issues on which the mainstream media had not put him to the test.

The 2008 Election and the Rise of Netroots

Remarkable developments in the arena of online political engagement transformed the dynamics of the 2008 election so that average people's money, perspective, and input counted more than ever politically. These changes will accelerate in the 2010 midterm election and beyond with the explosion in 2009 of social media.

Here's a snapshot of what occurred.

The new "public financing" became small money over big money and taxpayer money. Obama's online, small-donor fund-raising gave him a critical edge over Senator Hillary Clinton in the 2008 primary and allowed the grassroots or "netroots" to overcome the most powerful Democratic political machine in modern history, the Clintons. The small-donor netroots engine meant that Obama raised more money from more donors in a single quarter than any presidential candidate in modern history. The candidate's Web-based online community, "MyBo," helped Obama raise more than $200 million in donations of less than $200 each during the Democratic primary. Obama's

Internet fund-raising also changed the paradigm for what is the gold standard of campaign finance cleanliness. Obama rejected public financing, taxpayer money, in favor of allowing small-donor money to drive his campaign. Senator McCain, the author of the landmark McCain-Feingold campaign law, had a difficult time getting traction for his criticism of Obama's prolific Internet fund-raising. After all, Obama was accountable to millions of donors. What was more populist: taking public funds or taking the public's funds?

With the Supreme Court's weakening of state public financing laws in 2008, in a decision that neutered Arizona's landmark public financing law, the small-donor Internet money machine is likely to be the new standard for populist "clean money" politics in the future. Having badly lost a 2006 ballot initiative for public financing of statewide officials in California, I can say from experience that the public has always had a difficult time with public financing proposals because they don't like paying for politicians they generally don't like. The Internet small-donor program lets the public finance whom they really like by giving them choices that a taxpayer program denies them. It's the true new definition of "public financing" based on the most saleable principle in politics: more choice.

The Internet is the new "public eye" from which the public can cast a more informed judgment and move beyond misleading thirty-second television advertising and sound bites on the news. When candidates, public officials, or other public figures make a major gaffe, the public now has a new way to look at it, discuss it, and respond to it. YouTube video provides a 24-7 window into political moments and gaffes, and a stage for biting satire and other relevant commentary. For example, Senator Hillary Clinton got a second life in the 2008 Democratic primary when she teared up in responding to a question about campaign stress at a New Hampshire restaurant. The public went online to decide for itself whether she was authentic, viewing from every angle on YouTube.

Senator Obama's first salvo against Senator McCain regarding his involvement in the Keating savings and loan scandal came in the form of a thirteen-minute video to his supporters detailing McCain's involvement. The case could not have been made as eloquently in a thirty-second advertisement, yet 770,000 Americans watched that piece on YouTube in the first twenty-four hours of its being posted. The short exposé came on the eve of the second presidential debate and served as a warning to McCain, who had been making waves in the media about attacking Obama personally to close a widening gap. The Keating video laid out from the perspective of a banking regulator what McCain did wrong and why the senator was among the "Keating Five" who were admonished by the Senate for questionable judgment.

Political supporters can organize themselves for action. New technology during the 2008 presidential campaigns allowed for virtual phone banks and offline organizing using online means. Volunteers signed in online and received the numbers of neighbors to call for get-out-the-vote efforts, or were given the addresses of local doors to knock on. Such neighbor-to-neighbor word of mouth is the most highly effective political communication in a world overwhelmed by manipulative branding and advertising. The online effort to organize in the real-life world helped drive hundreds of thousands to the polls in critical primaries for Senator Obama, an edge Senator Clinton could never match because she had no comparable effort. The online edge proved critical for Obama in the general election too.

You don't need a television network or television advertising campaign budget in order to influence a political debate. Robert Greenwald has pioneered the use of his new media company, Brave New Films, which creates online films, videos, and social media forums, to educate tens of millions of people about *The Real McCain* and deliver other political messages. His grassroots but professionally produced online videos shaped public opinion about the election in ways the candidates themselves could not—explaining why doctors were concerned about McCain's failure to disclose his health records and risk of cancer reoccurrence, giving Americans a glimpse of the angry side of McCain, exposing McCain's many homes, and showing how Fox News race-baited Michelle Obama. Greenwald's editing of video clips and masterful directing helped steer the presidential debate in ways previously impossible on a small budget. In the same way, Greenwald had earlier captured Fox News commentator Bill O'Reilly's uglier moments in a montage that discredited the conservative commentator. Greenwald's Brave New Films scored big points after the election with videos against the war in Afghanistan, against the greed of health insurance companies, and for fairness in the media. Allies inside and outside of government used his frame of attack in the cause of progress. Robert recommends every public interest group have its own "one-man band," a person who can film, edit, and put video on the Internet to further its cause.

The nature of instant political communication lets the public have direct daily communications with powerful leaders. Candidate and campaign blogs let the public inside campaigns. E-mails from candidates maintain daily contact with supporters, raise money for special projects, and mobilize outpourings of support to influence others. Barack Obama wrote personal e-mails to his followers before and after key debates. His campaign manager, David Plouffe, taped special video updates for followers that were e-mailed to them. The Obama campaign had a way of making every supporter feel as though he or she was a major donor.

Campaign supporters have their feedback heard in unprecedented ways, too, thanks to how good ideas spread from the bottom up. Consider this story from Knoll Lowney about how e-mail from his wife Barbara Flye ended up taking on a big role in the presidential campaign. I campaigned with Barbara when she directed a consumer group in Washington State, so I have no question about its veracity. Here's some of the e-mail Knoll circulated:

> Subject: Barb Flye v. John McCain (Low Priority, but Fun Story)
>
> Barb picked up a magazine for insurance actuaries in her office because it had articles on health insurance by McCain and Obama. She saw a beautiful quote from John McCain, which could not have been more timely:

"Opening up the health insurance market to more vigorous nationwide competition, as we have done over the last decade in banking, would provide more choices of innovative products less burdened by the worst excesses of state-based regulation."

When she showed it to me, I agreed this was important, so on Thursday (9/18) we sent it off to our friend Jenn in NYC, "who knows people." One of those people (who happened to be a friend of Barb's) sent it to Paul Krugman at the *New York Times* and on Friday night reported to Barb that the quote was moving.

As it turned out, Krugman blogged about the quote on Friday (9/19). Almost instantaneously, it becomes the top story on Huffington Post and Daily Kos. When we checked Saturday morning, about four thousand readers had commented about the story on these two Web sites alone. "Kos," one of the most well-known and influential progressive bloggers, wrote, "Now, in this brilliant little passage in an obscure journal for actuaries, John McCain has just admitted that he was part of the group of people who brought us the Wall Street mess."

One comment said the Obama people had to get this quote, and Kos himself reported that they had it. Lefty and democratic blogs everywhere were writing about it throughout Friday night and continue to do so.

Then, Saturday morning, Obama started using the quote in his stump speech as a central attack on McCain.

In Florida, Obama said: ... "So let me get this straight— he wants to run health care like they've been running Wall Street. Well, Senator, I know some folks on Main Street who aren't going to think that's a good idea."

Prior to the super-conductivity of information on the Internet, no ordinary citizen, other than a major campaign donor, had this type of real-time access to a presidential candidate.

Obama's Missed Internet Opportunity

Of course, the challenge for progressives is putting such tools to good political use after elections. "Technology enables insurgency more than an institutional hold on power," explains national blogger Jerome Armstrong.

President Obama is the first president of the Internet era to communicate regularly with millions of supporters through personalized e-mails and videos. Obama also deserves credit for an unprecedented amount of online transparency at the White House. His new media team created Webcam broadcasts of key legislative and cabinet meetings, live blogging of presidential events, and video and blogs by top staff on hot-button issues, and they put the White House on Facebook and in the social media world. The White House gets how to use the technology; where it's failed is in communicating more authentically with its audience. That may be the nature of governing, rather than campaigning. Still, the president made major missteps that relate back to his unwillingness to maintain his voice and perspective as an outsider. Running the White House and using the Internet to raise hell don't seem to be compatible for him. The hope had been that Obama would use the Internet as FDR had the radio for his fireside chats to reach the American people directly on emotional issues that official Washington wouldn't budge on. That just didn't happen.

The Obama campaign was so successful at online rabble rousing because it connected to progressive voters and personalized the political experience. Obama's online organizing chief was one of the Facebook founders, then twenty-four-year-old Chris Hughes, who created the strategy. The *New York Times* reported, "As supporters started to join MyBo in early 2007, Mr. Hughes brought a growth strategy, borrowed from Facebook's founding principles: keep it real, and keep it local. Mr. Hughes wanted Mr. Obama's social network to mirror the off-line world the same way that Facebook seeks to, because supporters would foster more meaningful connections by attending neighborhood meetings and calling on people who were part of their daily lives. The Internet served as the connective tissue.

While many candidates reach their supporters through the Web, the social networking features of MyBo allow supporters to reach one another." The site offered every user a personal account with her own blog, profile, network, fund-raising page, and event-planning software. On issues, users were offered the opportunity to speak their mind, to organize affinity communities (like environmentalists, African Americans, etc.), get their friends involved, act locally, and research issues. The online conversation drove checks into the bank, people into the street, and a community online for real-world support.

After the presidential inauguration, Obama didn't keep his thirteen-million-member e-mail list independent of the political establishment but turned it over to a project of the Democratic National Committee. Organizing for America (OfA), the party project, has tried its hardest but it hasn't mobilized the masses in ways that have moved debates forward. How can you go after the Democrats who stand in the way of the president's campaign platform when you are owned and operated by the party that they belong to?

For example, Senators Max Baucus and Ben Nelson, obstacles to ambitious health care reform, couldn't be attacked by OfA on the eve of the crucial Senate deliberations on health care because they were Democrats. OfA even promised early on that it would not lobby Congress. Though it broke that pledge later in the heat of health care reform, after Obama gave up most of what his base would want to fight for anyway, the concession to politicians spoke volumes to those of us on the list who paid attention. It's up to progressives to fill the vacuum, but the challenge is rousing a base generally supportive of the president to be antagonistic to his positions when it becomes necessary. It's one thing to sign up online for off-line hell-raising during an electoral campaign but quite another to push the government you elected to go further once it's over.

During the darkest days for health care reform, after Obama gave away the public option to the private market, as well as "Plan B" for lowering the age of Medicare recipients to fifty-five, populism 2.0

from the left and the right converged. The netroots pounced from both sides of the equation, and public opinion for the legislation deflated right as the insurers, employers, and GOPers were ramping up their own platforms.

The reality of the Internet age is that mistakes, like Obama's, can be creatively and exponentially amplified. The Internet is the last populist frontier, and its power to turn the tide of public opinion against cash-rich political and economic titans is a great weapon. The health care reform plan went back on track only after Democratic allies pounded on news of Anthem Blue Cross's 39 percent premium increases in concert with the president and public interest groups like ours in the traditional media. The outrage sparked new enthusiasm off-line and online.

Authenticity and Activism in the New(est) Virtual Frontier

With the U.S. Supreme Court opening the door to unlimited corporate funding of political campaigns, corporate messages and messaging will be ubiquitous online. But the platform of the Internet will be swayed less by money than by authenticity because there is a glut of money and a deficit of authenticity. You cannot just buy support on the Internet the way powerful political and economic interest groups can on television. As it has evolved, the Web and social media are among the last places where truth, real human truth, matters more than money.

To exploit online opportunities for making change, it's worth exploring briefly the way the Internet and social media have changed in recent years to better meet popular demands and needs, as well to become an even bigger reflection of popular opinion. That includes moving people to take to the streets when it's necessary.

The Internet is no longer simply a massive clearinghouse for information at the click of a mouse, or a lecture hall where users have endless choices of courses and channel. "Web 2.0" principles, and the social media revolution they have spawned, have turned the lecture hall into a town square, where users define the forum and the content. We now create the media, the online conversation, and that increasingly spurs political action off-line. As my Consumer Watchdog colleague Kent McInnis puts it, "Evolving user expectations for what constitutes a trusted and truthful online experience has forced producers to put much more faith in the collective wisdom and knowledge of the crowd. Allowing site visitors to supplement, if not create, a site's knowledge base is increasingly considered more trustworthy than those sites which continue to operate under Web 1.0's authoritarian principles."

The old Internet allowed individuals quick access to information that otherwise might have taken weeks to assemble. But the new Internet and social media space that surrounds it allow action based on that information in ways that lend a new power to public opinion (see table 3). At the most basic level, rating articles with stars, sharing them with a friend, offering a comment to a blog, and watching a video are simple ways to vote for a point of view. The angry mob builds quietly online and assembles off. Increasingly, social media have been a pivotal flash point for the Tea Party, as well as progressives.

One of the prevailing concepts in the new 2.0/social media conversation is a concept called the "wisdom of crowds." The sociological principle holds that the many are smarter than the few. Groups make better decisions than an expert, assuming the right diversity within a group. As this principle continues to evolve into new Internet functions, sites and media that amplify the pulse of public opinion will allow for more massive mobilizations in a way

Table 3. Web 1.0 vs. Web 2.0	
Internet Past	**Internet/Social Media Future**
Authoritarian	Communal
Information dissemination	Content creation
Wisdom of elite	Wisdom of crowd
Top-down/expert	Bottom-up/public consciousness
Closed source/proprietary	Open source/public domain

that can strike at established political power with new populist energy. For left and right, political development and mobilization will increasingly snowball on social media.

Web 1.0 was a platform that passed information down from the elite to the masses. Web 2.0 is a platform that allows the mob to create and to rule. As such, it is particularly dangerous for politicians who get on the wrong side of the stone throwing. The downside is that the creation of content by so many users can further fracture and disperse the public's attention. On the positive side, the well-aimed stone throw can hit its mark and inspire others.

Online, 2.0 populists now have a platform to mobilize not just by tapping into the energy of like-minded leaders and propelling it further, but also by exposing new scandals, confronting new villains, and changing unaddressed problems. For leaders and followers the opportunities to grow populist energy, propel a strong narrative forward, and close the deal on change are unprecedented.

Half of the top twenty Web sites in America at the start of 2010 were driven by user-generated content or social media and networking. In 2005, only two of these sites, MySpace.com and eBay, were in the top twenty most trafficked Web sites in America. Not surprisingly, the new online conversation and interaction have led to more off-line protests and rabble rousing.

Grassroots Movements Online

MoveOn organizes its online members for local events, house parties, and demonstrations to push causes like climate change and health reform that its own members vote to take on. The e-mail invitation for the local house party always comes from one of your neighbors. All politics is local, after all, even on the Internet. MoveOn is so successful because it takes on discrete campaigns, asks only one thing at a time, always updates its members on the results of its campaign, and constantly seeks input from its people. The authenticity of the conversation is critical to driving real-world results, which all online actions do in one way or another.

The Tea Party uses online organizing to turn out its adherents with great effectiveness. Key Tea Party Web sites like Teapartypatriotslive .org funnel followers to the latest rally or road show. Teapartypatriots .org connects you to your local Tea Party group and won't even let you in the site initially without asking you to sign up. The Tea Party, like MoveOn, is looking for real-world bodies and the real dollars for the fights they choose. The Tea Party organizes, like MoveOn, around hot-button news hooks and issues to make its case. Event calendars, group-loyalty features like "Tea Party Patriot of the Month," and a steady stream of propaganda about the latest government outrage feed a vital online community motivated to turn out off-line. The online applications and conversations drive the Tea Party and shape the face it shows publicly. Urgency, immediacy, and deadlines become concrete online, and these are replacing the less-immediate and less-urgent methods of direct mail and robo-calling that conservative groups traditionally relied on.

Born in the social media, the Coffee Party USA has become a progressive political movement in opposition to the Tea Party. With the slogan "Wake Up, Stand Up," filmmakers and activists Annabel Park and Eric Byler started a Facebook group in January 2010 that has turned into a real-world movement. Annabel's Facebook posting reads, "Let's start a coffee party . . . smoothie party . . . red bull party . . . anything but tea. geez. Ooh, how about cappuccino party? that would really piss 'em off bec it sounds elitist . . . let's get together and drink cappuccino and have real political dialogue with substance and compassion." The Coffee Party's progressive philosophy that government exists to reflect the collective will of individuals and is not oppressive, as Tea Partiers believe, drew 155,000 fans in the first six weeks. The first Coffee Day, with hundreds of coffee house events on March 13, 2010, helped build the Coffee Party's numbers. The fact that the young Coffee Party's Facebook statistics have eclipsed those of the Democratic National Committee's Organizing for America and the Tea Party shows how quickly a political movement can grow online from humble beginnings.

For progressives, opportunities to rouse public opinion online, as Park and Byler did, boil down to

1. Finding a niche and platforms that fit our needs and talents;
2. understanding how to craft, identify, and propel an effective populist message and narrative; and
3. seizing political opportunities by deciphering and puncturing the often archaic political code of deception and distraction that surrounds political decisions in America.

The Coffee Party succeeded because it tapped into an anger among progressives and tried to put it to constructive use. The founders chose Facebook as their platform and began a dialogue. For those wanting not to start a group but simply to add their influence, the equation is still the same. We all have to figure out how best to tap into the new online conversation and interaction to achieve our goals, and where we fit into overall movements based on that changing landscape. The process is constantly evolving.

CHAPTER FOUR

BUILDING YOUR OWN POPULIST 2.0 PLATFORM

When discussing how to construct a 2.0 platform to get your campaign goals across, it's good to bear this fact in mind: the rules of engagement are more about human tendencies and preferences than about building the medium. Focus on how, when, and where to throw stones, not just the technical dimensions of the slingshot. Influencing change online or off-line is much the same. The Internet simply provides a low-cost, immediate medium to communicate.

The goal of e-advocacy is simple. It's all about finding ways to use your opinions to trap other people's like-minded opinions and drive them with collective force at the source of a problem. The tools at our disposal continue to evolve, but each of the basic platforms has its advantages and challenges. Here is my take on the power and limitations of the main platform tools in a populist political campaign.

Blogs

The blog, or Web log, is a tool for experts and opinion rousers to weigh in and grow an audience, generally of opinion leaders and other aficionados more than mass followers, on a specific area of expertise or a particular political viewpoint. Consumer Watchdog launched Oilwatchdog.org as a blog in the spring of 2007 to provide insider news and analysis on the oil industry. It received about thirty thousand visits per week, mostly from opinion leaders in the media and legislative staff, but it also deciphered for the public the archaic code of oil-industry maneuvers and gas price changes. The Daily Kos political blog, founded by Gulf War veteran Markos Mouitsas Zuniga, has more than 1 million readers a day, and its niche is crushing conventional political wisdom with his progressive perspective and those of his followers—as well as amplifying the exposures of Americans like Barb Flye. Zuniga says, "To create long-lasting change in democracy, you must shape public opinion by making your voice heard, your ideas clear and your cause visible. In today's world, that means you manage modern media—not just its technology, but its gatekeepers, too, by bypassing, crushing or influencing them."

Blogs abound, and they are highly effective as a means to shape and propel opinions about our opponents and the mistakes they make, often through personal passionate expressions that resonate. The Huffington Post, Arianna Huffington's brainchild, is one of the top Web sites on the Internet because it uses the voices of the famous, well versed, and articulate in blog form to drive progressive public opinion against the enemies of progressives. The banner headlines every day are a talking-points list from the latest news hooks. Talk-radio hosts, politicos, and gossips of all types flock to the Huffington Post to refine and shape the opinions they propel into the world. Arianna's real-time news and online conversation receives more visitors than any newspaper Web site except the *New York Times:* 42.6 million in June, 2010.

For me one of the greatest aspects of a blog is the historical moments it can preserve. At ArnoldWatch.org, our group's watchdog blog on Governor Schwarzenegger's special-interest ties, the index of web logs (http://www.arnoldwatch.org/blogs/index.php) chronicles the twists and turns of the Gov's entire tenure from inauguration on.

With WordPress, an open-source software, anyone can create a blog, though it's best to have something to say that's unique and sustainable. The most important rules I have learned about blogging are to speak passionately from the heart, be consistent in how often you post, and be salient. The wisdom of the crowd will notice.

Social Media

Facebook, Twitter, Linked-in, MySpace, and other social utilities allow us to connect and share with other people in our network a "live feed" of information about our lives and beliefs through videos, photos, statements, and our joining of affinity groups. For those interested in social change, fanning public opinion can be every effective in the circles and networks one creates on a social utility like Facebook because peer-to-peer communications are the most effective and resonant.

Word of mouth is the most credible form of information, and social media makes it fly. Posting a video, linking to a Web page, or joining a group can have an exponential impact if peers notice and fan the opinions out to their networks. While mass e-mails from non-peers go unopened or are not acted upon, posts on closed social networks are noticed. Successful online social networks have the ability to create buzz and shape popular opinion in new and profound ways. The social networking capacity of Facebook allows the sharing of compelling information and calls to action between networks of friends. It can turn a virtual whisper campaign into an outpouring of popular opinion. That's how students managed to stop an overdraft fee hike by the bank UBS; there was an uprising on Facebook that got the bank's attention. Viral marketers of commercial products have found their tipping points on Facebook too, but the real potential for political movements comes from the reverberations that such networks capture with each action and reaction in a campaign for change.

Theo Yedinsky runs Social Stream Media and is a social media guru on the cutting edge of the political deployment of the technology. Yedinsky offers the following short analyses for the political uses of each of the major social media tools.

> **Twitter:** "The fastest message accelerator in the world that allows you to customize the conversation you want to follow online."
>
> **Facebook:** "The world's largest social network, enabling you to create a community of advocates along with large-scale use of the most powerful method of communication in the world—a message from a trusted friend."
>
> **YouTube:** "A global platform that gives anyone the ability to embed and share video content."
>
> **Slide Share:** "A community connecting and sharing around power-point presentations."

Scribd.com: "Using the power of social networking tools to connect and share around white papers and in-depth information."

Ning/Proprietary Social Networks: "Creating personalized social networks tailored to the needs and goals of an organization."

UStream: "Creating real time, interactive, online, live video streaming content that builds on the online video revolution pioneered by YouTube."

E-Mail

If the blog is about throwing stones, the mass e-mail is about gathering giant snowballs to roll over one's opponents. A well-crafted e-mail from the right author at the correct time can gather a lot of momentum. We have all been spammed to death, and "open rates" for mass e-mail decline by the moment. The key elements of an effective e-mail are (1) targeting an outrage; (2) speaking simply; (3) getting to the point, or the link to an action, quickly; (4) having it written by a known person or peer; and (5) having a provocative subject line like "Outrageous!" "Wow," "Disgusting," "We Cannot Let Them Do It," "Finally!" "Unbelievable," or "We Won!"

Which messages resonate—or in Internet terms are "viral" or "contagious"—is the subject of much debate. Generally, I believe that communicating effectively on the Internet is no different than making a popular flyer for a telephone pole. Persuasive writing is just that.

The key elements of a powerful message begin with authenticity. There must be a compelling, identifiable voice that grabs the reader's attention. And there must be an outrage to respond to.

Here are some of the best first lines from e-mails that have resonated effectively with my consumer group's list of one hundred thousand subscribers. To give credit where it's due, a crash course from one of the godfathers of Internet activism, Zack Exley, turned our response rate up significantly. Exley became infamous when candidate George Bush dubbed him "the Garbage Man" for sling-ing stones about the president during his first run for office. That recognition, of course, only grew Exley's platform.

"I almost fell out of my seat when I saw Intel's new advertising campaign. It shows six bowing African American athletes before a chino-clad, oxford-shirted white manager with the slug: 'Maximize the power of your employees.'"

"I could feel my blood pressure rising when I heard Hillary Clinton respond on the *Today* show to my comment about her in *Newsweek*."

"I almost crashed my hybrid when I heard the Environmental Protection Agency had killed California's tough new auto emission standards."

How can an effective e-message muster a movement? It can exploit the mistake by an opponent of change to rally public opin-ion, be it a racist act by a brand-name company, a politician's stupid remark, a government agency's gaffe, or a powerful leader's pettiness. The first line in such e-mails should get readers' blood boiling and make our opponent's mistake the issue.

Exley argues that mass e-mail is overused and that communicat-ing only when there is really something vital to say makes for credi-ble messages that rate big responses. Many of these kinds of first lines have become overexploited, too. The next great first line, though, or subject line, will be based on someone's emotional response to a development in a movement for change. And of course the rest of the communiqué needs to back it up based on the principles of effective e-communication. In general, the rule is be real and responsive. Create art, don't recite science. Table 4 illustrates how to be an effective communicator.

Given how slick and visually rich e-mail communications have become, the most effective e-mails and posts are often the simplest and most human. It's as though the public is looking through the technology for a real, genuine human voice. I have found that text-only e-mails that resemble a person-to-person e-mail have the best chance of breaking through the spam filtering of readers. Barack Obama adopted this style in his preelection e-mails to supporters

Table 4. Effective Online Populist Political Communication	
Persuasive	**Less Persuasive**
Personal and emotion-based	Dispassionate and slick
Responsive to an outrage	Raison d'etre is not focused on rallying a response
Opportunistic	Not opportunity-based or time sensitive
Has hyperlinked research to back up claims	Does not back up assertions and claims
Provides action link in beginning of e-mail	No call to action, or action link is too late
Specific and concrete	General
Short as possible	Longer than necessary
Has a point of view	Written in third person
Authentic	Non-revealing, boilerplate

with great effect. After the second presidential debate, Obama's text-only, graphics-free message started simply, like this:

> From: Barack Obama
> To: Jamie Court
> Subject: What did you think?
> Jamie—
>   I thought the differences between John McCain and me were pretty clear tonight.

Of course, Obama wanted a little money. And he ended, "Thanks, Barack."

As technology gets better and better at stylizing Internet communication, authenticity is valued more and more in online communication because it cuts through the spin, sale, and promotion to speak directly to users. Politics hungers for authenticity. It's a key reason Obama's campaign platform didn't have the same effect once he arrived in the White House. President Obama became an official voice, rather than a personal one. If the new social media is an online conversation, then, like any dialogue, it better be authentic, or it won't be interesting.

The Holy Grail for Change

The power of organizing through social media has the potential to change the world. Not only do these media enable campaigns to go viral in ways never before imaginable, but they also have breathed new life into some old campaign tools.

Boycotts were passé for the last three decades, because they were so hard to spur. Social media has made them effective almost overnight. Individuals can flex the power of their wallet and protest corporations with remarkable results. Look at the fate of Whole Foods, after its CEO John Mackey made the mistake of making disparaging remarks about Obamacare early in 2009, when it was still popular. Whole Foods customers, generally progressive, flexed their wallet and refused to buy the overpriced whole food based largely on social organizing through social media. Wholeboycott. com claims the boycott is the reason that Mackey stopped serving as chairman of the board of directors, even though he retained the CEO title. The vibrant Facebook community of boycotters continues, at the time of publication, to hold boycotts and actions in different cities. Boycotts and protests had been hard to pull off because of the costs and difficulty of paying for mass communications. Now you can leverage online media and social networks to effectively hold corporations accountable. This has a big ripple in politics. No other retail company stood up to fight Obamacare after the progressive reaction against Whole Foods.

Social media also helped spur the growth of the "flash mob," a large group of people who assemble in a public place to perform a public act, then disperse. Viral e-mails, social networks, and texting gather a flash mob. The tactic was put to great political use recently in San Francisco where a flash mob production, complete with gay singers, dancers, and orchestra, assembled in the lobby of the Saint Francis hotel to perform a hilarious rendition of Lady Gaga's "Don't

Get Caught in a Bad Hotel," to support a strike by hotel workers. The YouTube video of the flash mob became an instant hit, spread like wildfire, and inspired protests at the hotels on the "bad hotel" list.

Brands, like a hotel chain, can be hurt where it matters through social organizing, even if you don't move the dial greatly on how many rooms a hotel rents or products a company can sell. In an era when the public brand is the coin of the realm, tainting the brand is a huge hit against a corporation. The social media platform makes these corporate giants vulnerable to one creative act or particularly egregious horror story. Go after the company where it hurts, as we did with Yahoo. Find out what it is that a corporation wants for its own financial gain—and target it like a laser. It may be a specific policy in DC or at the state level. It may be a project in a different country. It could be investments from public pension funds. Identify something that they want and go after it, because once you begin hurting something that impacts their business, they get very nervous. That's when they concede to reform.

A recent example from my files is our campaign against Google. When we launched a project in August 2008 to educate Americans about Google's privacy problems, the Internet goliath had a credible mantra, "Don't Be Evil," and a brand that seemed impenetrable. Despite cornering the Internet search and advertising market, and tracking our every move online, so that it can serve us up to its advertisers, Google's lack of concern for Americans' privacy had largely evaded the eyes and anger of Americans and regulators. Fast-forward two years. Due to our Internet and social media organizing about Google's privacy problems, the "Don't Be Evil" motto had become a popular punch line for a joke. The Justice Department joined us to try to scuttle Google's digital books deal, which as originally conceived would have given Google a monopoly over the world's digital literature and direct knowledge of all our reading lists to sell to advertisers. Google also had to pull out of a joint advertising alliance with Yahoo owing to government concerns about the monopolistic power of its search engine. The Federal Trade Commission and Congress were looking into regulating online "behavioral advertising," and Google responded to this scrutiny by offering new privacy controls and encryption security in its services in direct response to Consumer Watchdog's criticism and to avoid government action. We pulled the curtain back on Google's privacy problems with a laserlike focus on Google's biggest business priorities. Now consumers know how Google has tracked them across the Internet, stole information from private Wi-Fi networks with its street-view cars, and turned private e-mail addresses on Gmail accounts into public social networks on its Buzz service.

Of course, the company itself helped us with some big mistakes. One was to contact the Rose Foundation, a charitable organization that funded our privacy project, to ask that it not fund us anymore. The Google executive even put the suggestion in an e-mail, which we spread widely to the media, after receiving it from the foundation. The online world responded to the irony; this was hardly a testament to Google's "Don't Be Evil" motto.

Simple Rules of Engagement for Successful Social Media Campaigns

Social media offer tremendous opportunities for each of us to put the public back in public policy and raise some hell around an outrage. Exposing a company's misconduct and confronting it publicly is often the best way to push a policy change forward in government. Once elected officials see a big abuse, politicians often want to make a name by becoming reformers.

Americans who want to do their duty can see their role this way:

1. Connect to your platform and build it.
2. Wait for your opponent's mistake.
3. Rally opinion about the mistake through your platform and social network.

The critical mistakes that the powerful opponents of change make can be vastly amplified on the Internet in ways the traditional media never would for fear of looking biased or, more likely, out of a concern for losing access if they burned a powerful source. Journalists who run too many negative stories about a governor or president suddenly find themselves the last to hear about any news out of that office.

So what can the public do to, first, help create the record for change and, second, make a powerful opponent fearful of falling from grace if they don't succumb to reform?

1. Listen for important echoes and intensify them. When you hear Paul Revere in your e-mail, get on Facebook or Twitter and let your friends know the British are coming.
2. Make the mistakes the issue. The public is the crowd, the mob, the cheap seats in the bleachers. Our job is to provide the boos, the heckles, the jeers to make the political performers better at what they do. Opinion leaders can whisper all they want, but when the mob starts gathering at the doors the political aristocracy will start to make new laws if they remember their Marie Antoinette correctly.
3. Be an early adopter in the technology of the Internet political revolution. Exploit every platform that makes sense for you. Don't be timid; adopt early the online tools that can amplify your voice.
4. Show up. Showing up is more than half of the fight. Being in the right place at the right time is why reformers are able to leverage change. Securing an online platform can help more Americans fan the fires of public opinion when it counts. In my career, just being in the game often put me in the right place to change it, and this experience is common. It's particularly true when we also apply the fundamentals: read situations and people, anticipate the next move, then apply the jujitsu of populist power to achieve our goals. At the end of

this chapter are some charts that can help remind us of where we are in a change campaign and what needs to be accomplished at each stage.

5. Create your vision virtually and make it real physically. Whether it's the flash mob, the Coffee Party, or the political crusade, if you have a vision, throw it out on social media, then see what comes back. If you hit the sweet spot, chances are you will build something bigger and better than you ever dreamed for almost no money at all.

Finding and Using Messengers

Successful campaigns, be they for issues or candidates, need the three *M*s: money, messengers, and messages. The Internet can propel all three. Money may be the least important component of a modern change campaign given the power of social media. So let's focus on how Americans serve as messengers to grow memorable messages in a change campaign.

As we discussed in chapter 2, finding the right few people to influence is important. Successful social changes have hinged on finding those people who can connect to others and spread the word—even long before social utilities like Facebook or political utilities like MyBo made it ever easier to connect. While the ties are "weak"— acquaintance rather than sibling—they are far-reaching. Such connections and word of mouth can leave a big impression in the public consciousness because word of mouth is the most trusted source of opinion in a culture where slick marketing campaigns are ubiquitous.

In *The Tipping Point*, Malcolm Gladwell refers to these people as "connectors" and describes the other types of messengers who are particularly adept at moving change forward. They fall into these categories:

- Vigilantes: "If they find something amiss—a promotion that's not really a promotion—they'll do some-

thing about it. . . . These are the people who keep the marketplace honest."
- Mavens: "Someone who wants to solve other people's problems, generally by solving his own." A Maven is not a persuader. Their "motivation is to educate and to help. . . . Mavens are really information brokers, sharing and trading what they know."
- Salesmen: She has the "skills to persuade us when we are unconvinced of what we are hearing."

We all know some of these folks. It's not hard to see how the new online platforms can amplify the capacity of these types of messengers to be heard.

Closing in on Change

How does a campaign for change replete with each of these types of messengers accomplish its goals—moving from exposing an opponent, confronting him, waiting for his mistake, and exploiting that mistake—to the final outcome of change?

Successful movements for change move from one phase to another based on popular reactions. The modern Internet and social media space may be the best conductor for the current of popular opinion ever. Its capacity to spread and promote information about new exposures, confrontations, and mistakes was previously unimaginable in the political sphere. The real goal is to have a network replete with connectors, mavens, vigilantes, and salesmen who can serve their special roles in creating tipping points. Again, there's no formula for that art, but knowing the parameters and following your gut can further a change movement in a pivotal way.

What kinds of popular responses, fanned or provoked from your platform, can catalyze transformation of an issue from one phase of a change campaign to the next? Table 5 can help you see the more common ways popular opinion elevates campaigns for change.

Of course, when populist discontent begins to bubble up and

Table 5. How Popular Opinion Elevates Campaigns for Change	
Phase	**Popular Responses That Catalyze Change**
Exposure	Spontaneous expressions of outrage fan attention.
	Word of mouth makes the narrative more relatable and popularly identifiable in details as it spreads in society. The messengers make the story their own.
	New details fuel more expression of outrage, calls for disclosure, and whisper campaigns.
	Call for full disclosure becomes a popular drumbeat and consensus.
Confrontation	Demonstrable numerical showing of support for reformer (poll, petition, e-mails, Web hits, blogs, etc.).
	Opponent of change gets a black eye from the public and emerges with a negative public face.
Mistake	Opponent's base and constituency respond negatively—a company's shareholders, an elected official's constituents, or members to union leader.
	Opponent's allies are targeted and distance themselves for fear of fallout.
Mistake cascade/narrative becomes clear	Outrage gives rise to artistic expression that is more biting.
	Popular satires circulate.
	Mistakes become part of culture's lore: late-night television jokes, etc.
	Opinion leaders personally taunt opponent and target is provoked to take a stand for change.

threaten the political establishment, it will fight back—and hard. Table 6 lists the types of tactics that you can expect from the other side to foil change, and the jujitsu moves that can turn them around again.

In the end it's about the moves on the one hand, and the platform and the persistence of reformers on the other. Progressives are through

Table 6. Change and Counter-Change		
Tactic	**Reaction**	**Jujitsu**
Exposure	Denial	Call for full disclosure
	Designate scapegoat	Turn scapegoat into whistleblower; exploit new revelations
	Attack credibility of proponent	Rally proponent's supporters and allies: "Don't blame the victims"
	Confess and claim it is isolated incident	Call for full acceptance of platform for change as proof of regret
Confrontation	Lie	Call for independent investigation/audit
	Ignore allegations	Attack arrogance; demand accountability and response
	Attack critics	Rally allies
Force Mistake	Ask for forgiveness	Demand repentance
	Refuse to admit mistake	Create record
		Rally more supporters to your corner based on how out of touch opponent of change is
Mistakes cascade	Admit error/try to control reform	Demand nonnegotiable concessions
		Attack conflicts of interest and weaknesses in counter-change proposal

waiting for their president to act on the subjects of their outrage; they need to make their move so that their president and Congress act. While discreet issues, like privacy on the Internet by a specific company, may be more possible to tackle than acts of Congress on issues like global warming, every campaign for change is made of smaller campaigns. For example, Consumer Watchdog's campaign in 2007 to put the problem of health insurance rescissions—when insurers cancel coverage for innocent omissions in an enrollment application—on the map influenced the issue. It also created fodder for Congress in the national health care debate of 2009, which ended the practice federally. Take up an issue that you care about. Use your platform. You'll probably be surprised at how taking a stand influences great debates that you never thought it would.

CHAPTER FIVE

GETTING THE AFFORDABLE HEALTH CARE YOU VOTED FOR

It was August 2008 and I was sitting in Concord, California, behind a one-way, soundproof mirror, like a CIA agent monitoring an interrogation. My colleagues and I were eavesdropping on a focus group of ten San Francisco Bay–area women voters who were expressing their deepest fears prior to the "Year of Change" election.

The group of probable voters had been picked from the "muddled middle" by an opinion research firm our consumer group contracted with. No extreme right-wing or lefty politics. These were middle-income soccer moms, flight attendants, and teachers in the political center. They voiced a lot of fear, anger, and insecurity, mostly economic, and little consistent thinking. Just flash points of anger. They kept coming back to health care.

- "Insurance company people are making so much money."
- "Individuals cannot afford to pay for individual insurance."
- "Doctors are paid so little by insurers they don't spend any time with you anymore."
- "Every year something is taken away from your insurance policy, not added."
- "It's a shame our country just cannot figure a way out like other countries."
- "Health care system . . . *what* system?"

The other focus groups we held across California, composed of similar men and women, all exhibited the same symptoms and articulated the same gripes.

Had so many Americans ever been so angry at their health care system?

In fact, they had: in 1991, just before President Clinton botched health care reform in many of the same ways, and with some of the same people, that President Obama did during his first year (see table 7). Obama may have finally delivered a health insurance reform plan into law in the spring of 2010, but gripes from average Americans like those in our focus groups will only intensify under it. That is, unless progressives can organize an improvement before the law's implementation in 2014 to push reform further at the state and federal level. Doing so is probably the most crucial goal for the progressive movement in America.

When Obama called for health care reform at the launch of his presidency, progressives had great hopes for true, comprehensive health care reform. To many that had supported the new president, this meant moving America toward a single-payer system—the kind of model that, in many different forms, has worked tremendously well for developed countries around the world. Other progressives skeptical about the success of single-payer legislation had their hopes set on what became known as the "public option," which would have allowed Americans to buy into a government-run health insurance plan, much like Medicare, as an alternative to buying private health insurance. But, in the end, the administration's drive for bipartisan support, and its concessions to industry, weakened the legislation that ultimately moved forward. As a result, Obama's reforms didn't

Table 7. Americans on American Health Care		
	1991	2007
Believe system needs to be disbanded and rebuilt	42%	38%
Believe system serves needs and merits only minor alteration	6%	11%
Believe fundamental change is needed to improve salient flaws	50%	50%
Percentage of uninsured	13.8% (37.4 million)	15.8% (47 million)
Percentage of underinsured	Not available	29% (75 million)

deliver fundamental change to the system or eliminate the most fatal flaws that have been disappointing Americans for decades.

The reforms did put forth a few advancements. By 2014 new federal safeguards will ensure that losing your job doesn't mean you lose your health insurance—and that private health insurance companies will have to show us a little more respect. The greatest progress made by the new law is that people of low and moderate incomes will be eligible for generous taxpayer subsidies to buy health insurance by 2014. Critical insurance-company accountability measures in place by 2014 will also force health insurers to take all comers regardless of preexisting conditions, to sell only policies that cap out-of-pocket costs, and to base premiums on factors other than medical condition.

What Americans did not get, though, was a cost-effective, government-administered health care system—or even an option to purchase health insurance through the government. A single-payer proposal never even made it to the table. The public option became the progressive's last stand for progress in the legislation. But the watered-down proposals died in the Senate with President Obama acting more like a willing undertaker than an outraged advocate.

The real price for whatever progress the final federal law will deliver is a new requirement that all Americans have to show proof of health insurance by 2014, and private health insurance is at the moment the only option. If your employer doesn't pay for coverage, and you make too much for a government subsidy, you will have to buy a health insurance policy yourself or face tax penalties. That's a far cry from health care reform for those of us working on the issue for the last twenty years. We envisioned health care services being available to all for free covered by tax payments, not everyone having to buy a health insurance policy that might not even provide coverage when you are sick. Moreover, Obama failed to address the real problems with health care that Americans have struggled with for decades: profiteering at all levels, the need for fundamental cost controls, and the lack of even basic insurance-premium regulation.

You will have to buy health insurance, but the government doesn't even have the right to tell insurance companies how much they can charge for it, or if their rates are excessive. As a result, those who pay for health care—employers, taxpayers, or individuals—aren't going to be much happier with what they are paying or getting than they are today. What will be ended is the right of insurance companies to treat their customers and potential policyholders with total disregard—refusing to continue their insurance if they become seriously ill, or refusing to cover them for previously existing conditions.

What opens is a window of opportunity to force the government to control costs, more fully regulate insurance companies, and provide a public option to the private market. Since government owns the health care problem, progressives have leverage to force real fixes.

What Now?

The American public got a first-class education on health care reform during President Obama's year-long fight, supplemented by what the cruelty of the insurance market had taught them. That cruelty won't change, absent real improvements on the federal law, nor will the anger it breeds. And this creates a fertile base for progressives.

Most Americans now feel that they are underinsured. Workers with health insurance from an employer pay an average of $3,492 in premiums and $2,675 in out-of-pocket costs. Co-pays, deductibles, and out-of-pocket costs of all kinds have proliferated. The average health insurance premium for a family of four is more than $12,000 per year. Americans have been forced to pay more and more, while getting less and less. Obamacare, as constructed, cannot deliver affordable health insurance policies with generous benefits. Something's going to have to give if government is to deliver on its promises.

Listening to focus groups on health care, it's very clear that Americans have received an unwelcome education about the inefficiency, illogic, and foibles of the American health insurance system. The public is even more outraged at the venality of the political establishment that abets the medical-insurance complex. They don't like what they're paying for, or the politicians paid to protect the status quo. The level of hostility at the pillars of the health care system—insurers, drug companies, hospitals, and even doctors—is unprecedented. Even physicians, once the trusted oracles about health care changes for patients, are increasingly losing standing with a public frustrated about waiting too long and having too little time with doctors. Patients in the muddled middle recognize that the insurance system is tapping them dry and there are no regulations to protect them. Witness the support in a 2008 poll by my consumer group for changing the rules, opening up health care coverage to more patients and making the system fairer. The last column in table 8 shows whether the populist proposals we polled the public about were included in the final federal health care reform law signed by President Obama.

The legislation that passed the House of Representatives in 2009 reflected more of the popular principles in our survey than the final law signed by the president. At least that legislation—unlike the Senate legislation passed on Christmas Eve 2009—contained a public option, which had become the litmus test for many progressives of whether Obamacare would be true to the principles of change that Obama had outlined in his campaign. When the president backed the Senate plan, without the public option or an alternative expansion of Medicare to fifty-five-year-olds, the shock waves through his progressive base helped precipitate the low turnout of progressives in the Massachusetts Senate race in January 2010, a loss that put the brakes on more comprehensive reform. The Massachusetts debacle remains a valuable lesson for the Democratic establishment. And progressives must not allow Democrats to forget that unless progressive reforms go back on the table, progressive votes are far from guaranteed. Conciliation and capitulation by the president undermined the real source of his power, the base of Americans who shared his values and elected him to stand by them.

States have a lot of latitude to implement the federal law and will be stuck with many of its problems and costs unless state legislatures or

Table 8. Tenets of a Populist Proposal				
Proposal	Favor	Oppose	Favor margin	Included in Obamacare?
Allows anyone to buy the same health coverage available to elected officials.	81%	9%	+72%	No
Limits the amount patients must pay out of pocket when they get sick.	75%	18%	+57%	Yes
Requires insurers to sell policies to anyone regardless of health condition.	75%	18%	+57%	Yes, but also requires all Americans to purchase policies
Requires health insurers to justify premium increases and get approval from state regulators for rate increases.	71%	22%	+49%	No
Rolls back health care premiums by 20%.	66%	23%	+43%	No
Requires the state to subsidize the cost of health insurance for low-income people.	64%	27%	+37%	Yes

state ballot measures fix the problems Congress created. State regulation of insurance premiums, the choice of state public options to the private market, and greater accountability for insurance companies are all possible. Congress and the executive branch also must fix the problems they will have created through new laws, or the reins of the federal government are sure to change hands. These are demands best made first of public officials and candidates in the run-up to the 2010 midterm election, when the Democrats fear losing Congress. Our success will be determined in large part by whether we engage the public through the strategies outlined in chapter 1. Is our cause communicated in human terms? What is the moral sentiment behind it? How well do we expose and confront the opponents of our reforms, be they insurers or the politicians who accept their money, and force their mistakes? Our opponents, of course, must first be defined, and by now, progressives should have no question who they are.

Not the Change We Voted For

This is the most anticorporate environment in modern history, and yet the health insurance industry has occupied a central seat at the table on both ends of Pennsylvania Avenue. The industry's demand that all Americans be forced to buy private health insurance policies turned President Obama against his campaign promise of not imposing such a mandate to purchase private policies. The insurers' demand that the public not even have the choice of a public option won over the Senate and President Obama. Insurers are the enemy. Public opinion polls prove it. Obama lost a lot of public support for his health care positions because he spoke out of both sides of his mouth. Public Enemy No. 1 cannot be tarred and feathered in the court of public opinion, then allowed to write the reform plan in the back rooms of Congress and the White House. It's not authentic, and the public has perfect radar for the lack of authenticity.

Polls consistently show Americans have been very clear in their resolve for strong reforms of the insurance industry and a public alternative to it, but not for being forced to buy private insurance. My consumer group polled Americans on whether they should be required to buy health insurance, and only 16 percent supported the notion. Somehow, though, this is the centerpiece of the new federal law.

Remarkably, Presidents Obama and Clinton failed the public on health care reforms in fundamentally the same way, even though Obama has a law to show for it. They listened, pandered, and gave their loyalty to the insiders and forgot to represent the outsiders who put them in office.

President Clinton's health care plan failed for five key reasons.

1. The public was left out of the debate after the election.
2. The medical-insurance complex hijacked the process for its own ends, then turned on it altogether.
3. Complexity, to serve interest groups, won out over simplicity, which would have kept the public motivated.
4. In the absence of ownership over the process, the public was susceptible to fear-mongering by the insurers and drug companies that opposed change.
5. Insiders seeking reform forgot the power of the outsiders, the public, while opponents of reform harnessed public fear.

Without major modification, President Obama's law will fail, and for similar reasons:

1. He capitulated on the top priorities of the majority of Americans in order to appease insiders on Capitol Hill and K Street so that he could have legislation pass quickly.
2. He wooed the medical-insurance complex with concessions that abandoned key campaign promises and alienated the middle class because he feared moneyed opposition to a stronger plan would kill it.
3. The President focused on presenting complex policies to voters rather than on creating a simple narrative that would satisfy the public.
4. White House chief of staff Rahm Emmanuel's strategy of getting a bill at all costs regardless of the details, in order to avoid Clinton's failure, created legislation destined not to satisfy the public.
5. Instead of challenging members of his own party over their fealty to insurers, Obama refused to play hardball and test Capitol Hill insiders in the way that was necessary to represent outsiders and move a stronger bill.

Struggling middle-class Americans really care about a few key questions:

- Who will pay for health care?
- How much will they pay?
- What do patients get for the price?

Remarkably, despite the new federal health care law, these questions are still largely unanswered. Employers today pay the lion's share of most Americans' health insurance, so the individual mandate to buy insurance seems a lot less scary. The problem is that penalties under the new federal law for employers to pay for health coverage are relatively small. Employers with fewer than fifty employees don't have to provide health coverage, so employees for small businesses could well have to buy their own insurance. Small employers are typically the ones who don't provide coverage today. Large employers do, but under the new law the maximum penalty for an employer with more than fifty employees who doesn't offer insurance is $2,000 to $3,000 per employee. The penalties are less than half the current price of a standard health insurance policy for an individual. So big employers may choose not to pay for coverage, and individuals will have to buy their own policies. If the worker is too poor, the government will pay some or most of the cost. The problem is that it's not clear how much insurance policies will cost. Nothing in the federal law sets a cap on the prices of premiums or allows the government to veto excessive premiums.

In the spring of 2010, our consumer group filed the first comments on the first two regulations of the new health care law. The bizarre nature of the law came into sharp focus. The Department of Health and Human Services is empowered to review "unreasonable" rates, but it's unclear how regulators will know a rate is unreasonable since there is no review to determine what is reasonable. Plus the department can review, but has no power to deny, an unreasonable premium. Only the insurance industry lobbyists could produce legislation like that. There are formulas in the bill to determine the value of benefits and ratios between the least expensive and most expensive policies, but fundamentally no protections exist to make sure the policies' price isn't too high and the benefits aren't too low.

Americans' anger over the health care system is only going to grow without comprehensive reform that adequately answers these questions of cost, burden, and benefits. The road to real progressive reform is to plow ahead with new initiatives on the state and, when possible, federal levels that answer these questions for the public. Let's recall the tried-and-true principles for progressives that work: (1) keep it simple and give the public what it wants; (2) expose and confront the opponents of reform, in this case health insurers and drug companies; and (3) turn the debate inside out by bringing the outside in.

Turning the Debate Inside Out

One sunny morning early in January 2010 I found myself in Ronald Reagan country, near the epicenter of the devastating Northridge earthquake of 1994, in the tree-lined suburban community of Porter Ranch. I waited outside the home of Hilda Sarkysian, who lost her daughter to cancer at the age of seventeen after CIGNA denied a potentially lifesaving liver transplant. Waiting with me was the former CIGNA executive who handled public relations for the insurer in the case and then had a crisis of conscience.

Wendell Potter came onto the scene of health care reform suddenly the summer before. He called me first, before coming out as a whistleblower, and introduced himself. I warned him about the dangers for whistleblowers and the alienation they faced, but Wendell knew he could make a huge difference if he decided to come forward. After the handling of Sarkysian's case, Potter could no longer continue in his CIGNA job, and he retired at age fifty-six. He wanted to tell the world how health insurers really operate.

Wendell was nervous that morning. He had flown from his home in Philadelphia the night before just to see the family. Ever since that first call to me he had said he wanted to meet Hilda, and she, too, wanted to meet him. She had seen him on PBS's *Bill Moyers Journal* talking about his crisis of conscience over the family's case. This was the moment Wendell had waited for to make amends, but with repentance comes anguish. From inside the Sarkysian house, we got word that Hilda's husband and son were angry, and possibly not ready to meet Wendell. It was tense for a half hour or so until Wendell knocked on the door. We were waiting outside the home with two television cameras crews from *Dateline NBC* that I had arranged to capture the moment. We hoped the show would air before health care reform concluded so that the abuses in this case would be addressed by federal legislation.

When Hilda opened the door, the emotions ran very high. Over the next hour and a half, Wendell, Hilda, and the rest of the family were again and again reduced to tears. This was ground zero for American health insurance gone awry. Potter had been instrumental in getting CIGNA to approve the treatment for Nataline, Hilda's daughter, but his support came too late. Nataline died before she could get the transplant. As Hilda explained to Wendell, and later to the *Dateline* audience, she didn't even have an opportunity to say goodbye to Nataline. She was at a rally at CIGNA offices in Glendale fighting for her daughter's treatment when her lawyer whispered in her ear that she had been approved. Wendell was watching the scene on TV and had worked to get the news to the family. But Nataline died just hours later, unable to hold out any longer for the surgery. Not long after, Wendell resigned.

At the Sarkysians' home, Wendell was confronted with posters from the demonstration and pictures of Nataline, and he visited the seventeen-year-old's room. The transplant was the only chance she had had to save her life, and CIGNA delayed, probably because it knew that in the end it would face no real legal account-ability for the death. That morning in Porter Ranch, Hilda and Wendell agreed to fight together for changes in the law. For me, the emotion of their meeting was like the splitting of an atom. At that time, health care reform was seen as very likely to pass and be signed into law in weeks. There was hope that what we didn't get in that bill—real legal accountability for health insurers in cases like Nataline's—we could get later. After all, once the U.S. government and the Congress owned reform they would have to fix the holes and defects in it.

But the Massachusetts senatorial special election changed all that. By the time *Dateline* aired its hour-long episode of denied treatment for insured patients, the Democrats had lost their filibuster-proof supermajority, and Obamacare was on death watch. In his first State of the Union address, Obama took responsibility for failing to communicate health care reform appropriately and clearly to the American people and acknowledged that it looked like a backroom process. I only wonder what would've happened had Obama joined forces with either Wendell or Hilda earlier.

Wendell became the rock star of the health care reform movement from almost the moment he came forward at a U.S. Senate Commerce Committee hearing in June 2009. Yet he was not invited to the White House once during the reform effort, nor was Hilda, who had been featured before on national television too. By contrast the CEO of CIGNA, according to visitor logs made public by citizen's groups' requests, met with the president at least twice.

Outsiders like Wendell and Hilda should have been the messengers of real health care reform, not President Obama or Senate Finance Committee chair Max Baucus, whose critical roles in the mathematics of vote counting inside the Capitol made them the face of the effort for the public. The outsiders needed to be brought in for the insiders to turn outward.

Hilda and Wendell made a pact that morning in Porter Ranch to combine their power to create change. They are just a few of the faces and stories of the movement who embody and express the authentic moral sentiments that two-thirds of Americans agree with. President Obama and members of Congress would have lost some control if they had turned the debate over to Wendell and Hilda, but they would have gained power too, power to dictate the terms of the debate.

Hilda and Wendell's message is this: Just because you're insured doesn't mean you're covered. That premise is still true under the new federal health care reform law. Patients with employer-paid health insurance have no more legal rights than Hilda Sarkysian, who could not sue over Nataline's death because her husband's employer paid for her coverage. This needs to change and it will. The need for change comes from the heart of a mourning mother and speaks to the hearts of Americans.

Early in Year One, Consumer Watchdog worked, from our storefront near the Capitol, to focus on the fine print in insurance policies and how it hurts average Americans. We tried to humanize the debate with the stories of patients caught in the insurers' traps. We released internal insurer underwriting guidelines that showed that firefighters, police officers, steelworkers, expectant fathers, pregnant women, and patients with asthma, acne, allergies, and toenail fungus would not be sold individual health insurance policies because insurers blacklisted these patients in the absence of a "take all comers" law. I helped Wendell come out to the world because I knew the power of the story of an insider coming out would appall and resonate with Americans. Consumer Watchdog had also been instrumental in exposing insurers' practice of canceling patients' insurance right when they needed it most, when they were hospitalized or had racked up other big medical bills, due to innocent omissions on their enrollment applications. We helped bring those patients to Washington, D.C., to confront the insurance executives who made the decisions. Some of the best fireworks of the national health care reform debate in Year One came at a hearing where insurance executives acknowledged that they regretted canceling patients who did not intentionally lie on their enrollment applications, acknowledging that people would die because of it, but that they would continue to do so because the law allowed it.

One of the only bipartisan moments in the health care debate came when Joe Barton, a Republican congressman I had known for his allegiance to Big Oil, asked during the hearing if the executives had remorse. They said it bothered them, but they had to cancel honest applicants. All three executives refused to commit their companies to only canceling patients when they could show intentional fraud. "I think a company does have a right to make sure there's no fraudulent information," said Barton. "But if a citizen acts in good faith, we should expect the insurance company that takes their money to act in good faith also."

Moral sentiments like this transcend left-right politics and go to the heart of American values. That's why the final national health reform law included a provision that insurers have to prove fraud if they want to cancel an insurance policy. Still, this was one of only a handful of hearings during the entire health care reform debate in Year One in which company executives were grilled about company abuses. Exposure and confrontation inside and outside the Capitol were rare. Backroom meetings that left the public out were the rule. In fact, the debate tilted toward enactment of a health care law only when Anthem Blue Cross and parent Wellpoint were hauled before Congress to discuss a 39 percent rate increase in California. Obama used his platform and seized on the company's mistake to drive through the final legislation, even though nothing in the bill would prevent such a premium increase in the future.

Using Moral Sentiments to Reform Health Care

Confronting our opponents with strong moral sentiments—such as the fact that health insurers should not be able raise their prices 39 percent on a whim—is the path to real reform. Elected officials who oppose such sentiments will pay a price, and it is the job of progressives to put them on the spot.

The new federal law that passed largely embodied the following moral sentiments and included prohibitions on insurance companies that defied them.

- An innocent omission on an enrollment application shouldn't be a reason that anyone loses health coverage when he or she needs it most.
- Insurers should not be allowed to deny patients health insurance because they had toenail fungus, were a firefighter, or became a father.

- Patients should not be charged more for health insurance because they are sick.

America and Americans have a long way to go before health care reform is done right, but the campaign to improve the foundation established by Obama should center on these types of moral sentiments.

- Americans should not be forced to buy insurance that is not affordable and not regulated.
- Prescription drugs should be purchased in bulk by government programs in order for taxpayers to receive the cheapest price.
- Insured patients should be covered when they need their coverage the most, or insurers should pay a big price in court.
- States should give the public the right to choose a public health insurance system, rather than a private insurance market, if they have to buy health insurance as a condition of citizenship.

Reform should and will begin here. Whether the federal government passes some or all of these proposals, state legislatures are likely to lead the way on creation of insurance premium regulation, bulk-purchasing pools for prescription drugs, and public options to the private market. Under the new federal law, states are charged with setting up insurance exchanges, the places individuals go to get health insurance if their employer doesn't provide it. States have the ability to enact public options that don't use insurance companies. In California, for example, we have proposed opening up the state employees' retirement plan, which bypasses insurance companies, as a public option. Twenty-four states and the District of Columbia have ballot-measure provisions, through which citizens can ask voters to enact such laws directly. When the federal government passes a requirement that all Americans have to show proof of health insurance or face tax penalties, statehouses and state ballots are likely to quickly be filled with simple proposals like the ones above, and others, to rein in insurers.

Now that the government has decided to require private health insurance, government at every level will have an even greater moral obligation to fix what they have come to own. Mandatory auto insurance created the same window of opportunities in the states; auto insurance was required, but it wasn't affordable.

The most important of these state proposals would be a public alternative to the private health insurance market. Somewhere between 50 and 72 percent of Americans support the public option according to polls taken during Obama's first year, and if mandatory insurance were to take effect, the percentage of supporters would only grow. States have the capacity to enact these public options with waivers granted by the federal government to resolve the confusing employee and public assistance benefit issues. State legislatures and ballot measures that move such proposals along will likely find a willing White House.

Strategically the leap from important moral sentiments about fairness in a marketplace, which should garner bipartisan support from the public at least, to a comprehensive government substitute to the private market, with subsidies for those who cannot afford it and/or taxes subsidizing it, will take not only tactics but a change in vision as well. Obama and his partners in Congress, abetted by the liberal think-tank and private-foundation-funded cognoscenti, had not only bad tactics but a faulty product.

The Terms of the Debate:
Shared Risk vs. Shared Responsibility

The model for reform in the year of change was so-called shared responsibility. I have argued for a decade against the approach since I first heard it espoused in its infancy at a foundation-convened conference in Monterrey, California. At the time, California was flush with money, and it was clear that public sentiment had run hard against the health insurers, fueled in large part by our success-ful work on HMO reform at the state level. The question was what would be next. The representatives for the state's paper-tiger coali-tion of labor and social service groups said the best course was to go to the insurers, who knew they were unpopular, and work a deal to use the insurers' money for a scheme to get taxpayers to cover everyone who could not afford insurance, while requiring employ-ers to pay for the rest.

This was the beginning of the notion of "shared responsibil-ity," with the addition of a mandate for individuals to buy cover-age. Those of us who didn't trust private health insurers, and knew inevitable state budget deficits would return to kill such a program, argued for a "shared risk" model that created a single risk pool of all patients with a new government program, like California Medicare, and let private insurers participate if they added value. That sounded much too much like socialism for the foundation hosts, union pooh-bahs, and public interest propeller heads who made putting "shared responsibility" on the map their meal ticket.

My colleagues from Monterrey summed it up pretty clearly from the beginning. If the insurers have too much money to fight, why not join them? The prescription drug makers, who charge Americans 66 percent more than the rest of the world, won similar concessions for similar reasons from the liberal public-interest establishment in Washington, D.C., and ultimately from the White House.

It wasn't too hard to see that "shared responsibility" would fall hardest on taxpayers and individuals, because drug companies, health insurers, and employers had better lobbyists and gave away big campaign contributions. Obama won the White House in part by opposing mandatory health insurance for individuals and saying he would create bulk purchasing for prescription drugs, essentially leveraging "shared risk." He betrayed both promises, and it was a cost killer and public-opinion nightmare for the legislation.

If health reform is to succeed it must move toward the "shared risk" model and away from the "shared responsibility" frame. It's worth understanding both frames to see how they measure up.

Shared Responsibility

The "shared responsibility" approach touted by many insurers, employers, and some health care professionals focuses on who pays for health insurance, not how much they pay or what is covered.

Individuals, employers, and taxpayers all pay into the system. The focus is not on the kind of coverage or the size of the insurance risk pool, but on forcing the participants to pay—some with subsidy, others without. This is the core of the federal health care law. States are each charged with running their own health insurance exchanges, where individuals go to buy health insurance, rather than having a big national pool, which would be fifty times the size and more cost-effective, or a national public option to the private market. Economically, the smaller the pool, the more expensive the coverage and the fewer the benefits.

I have seen all the numbers on "affordable" individual policies based on the debates in California and Washington, D.C. What's clear is that any policy an American would consider affordable would come with huge deductibles, $5,000 or more, and such deductibles actually discourage appropriate use of health care, according to research. The mantra of "shared responsibility" comes down to "make the people pay whatever doctors, hospitals, and insurers want to charge."

The only real-world model for mandatory health insurance is the best evidence of the shared-responsibility paradigm's pitfalls. Massachusetts passed such a law, written largely by the medical-insurance industry, in 2006 and it took effect fully January 1, 2008. The Massachusetts law's successes in insuring lower-income residents are largely due to the fact that the state had a relatively small problem—about half a million uninsured to begin with. Its insurance providers are also largely nonprofit, unlike those of the rest of the nation. It is to the state's credit that it has offered health care—at substantial state expense—to people who couldn't begin to buy it themselves. But the unsubsidized portion of the plan has created anger and resistance among middle-class families left to the mercy of the private market. State budgets have swelled and deficits grown too because cost control was never in the equation.

Many of the previously uninsured, when polled, said the law has hurt them. The Harvard School of Public Health and the Massachusetts Blue Cross Blue Shield Foundation found support for the health care reform law, but those personally affected by the mandatory insurance, those forced to buy it, showed only 37 percent support for the state mandate. Forty-four percent of the previously uninsured said they were personally hurt by the law. The failure to create meaningful cost controls in the law has led to double-digit premium increases for those least able to pay—low-income residents who receive partial subsidies. The state budget has been devastated by the unwillingness to deal with cost controls, and taxes are on the rise. Taxpayers and individuals got it in the shorts.

Absent strict government regulation of what is appropriate for insurers, hospitals, and doctors to charge—the missing link in the new federal law—mandatory private insurance for all Americans can have only two possible outcomes: either prices will be prohibitive for consumers who have to buy insurance, or benefits will be so severely restricted that patients won't get the care that they need. It's almost impossible to mandate comprehensive benefits that cover most serious conditions for patients, as Medicare does, in a shared-responsibility program that gives so much latitude to the private insurers.

The shared-responsibility approach was developed as a consensus vehicle among medical "stakeholders" who understand the political imperative of having a plan to cover everyone. Most health insurers have jumped on the shared-responsibility bandwagon because they want to deflect attention from their role in the crisis.

What the health insurers want the public to forget is that 12 to 33 percent of every premium dollar they collect is eaten up by their increasing profits and overhead. The new federal law capped how much health insurers could take for profit and administration at 15 percent in the group market and 20 percent in the individual market, but keeping track of their accountants will be a full-time job for consumer groups like ours. Immediately after the passage of the law, major insurers began to recategorize their expenses to get around the requirements. Also, if insurers can take only 15 to 20 percent off the top, they have an incentive to allow for higher medical charges to boost premium costs, just like a Hollywood agent who gets more when his clients make more.

For the consumer, mandatory private health insurance proposals are all stick and no carrot. What we need is the carrot of affordable health care. That means the government should standardize charges by insurers, doctors, hospitals, and drug companies. No more $6 Tylenols in the hospital. Mandatory health insurance is a government bailout of a free market that's failed its customers. Fewer people and employers have been buying private health insurance because it costs so much more and delivers so little. So rather than let customers demand a new and better product, advocates of "shared responsibility" want to force us to buy it.

There are those who say it's harmful to tell a doctor, insurer, hospital, or drug company what's reasonable to charge. That it's socialism. Yet how reasonable is it to tell every American to buy a product whose cost is uncontrolled? Isn't that corporate socialism?

Americans are angry at the sway corporations have over their everyday lives, and they'll get more angry. It's time for health care reformers to take advantage of that fact by focusing on greater risk sharing.

Shared Risk

Sharing risk is the historical role of insurance: spreading risk across broad demographic groups in society—sick and well, old and young, rich and poor—so that no one individual bears the high cost of an unforeseen illness or catastrophe. Insurance pools were created so that you pay in when you are young and healthy, then take benefits out when you are older and/or sicker. Increasingly, health insurance has moved away from this model.

Health insurers have wanted to insure only the well and healthy, so they can make money by not paying claims. Such "cherry picking" has diced and shrunk the risk pools to smaller and smaller groups, rather than bigger pools that spread risk broadly. The industry has created boutique products for the young and healthy that are cheap yet profitable. They also removed these "good risks" from the larger pool and raised costs for the less young and not so healthy. Underwriting guidelines for the major insurers show that patients with minor ailments like heartburn and ulcers will not be sold coverage as individuals. The rules also facilitated one of the insurance companies' most reprehensible practices: canceling coverage for sick patients after they rack up medical bills, by combing their original insurance application for any omission or the most innocent error.

Patients who are part of group coverage, most commonly through an employer, don't have to submit to underwriting or face the threat of cancellation. But secure group coverage is shrinking. Patients too sick to work or recently laid off are forced to pay for costly continuation coverage (called COBRA), which varies in length after termination from a mere three months in Washington, D.C., to eighteen months in California. More and more are finding themselves uninsured and without the protection of a risk pool. National reform has established the role of government as ensuring that all patients have access to coverage and requiring insurers to keep the sick as well as the healthy on their rolls. The price and the benefits are what's at issue, and the bigger the risk pool, the better the deal on both. That's why it's incumbent upon progressives to push state governments to consolidate the risk pools into as great a pool as possible—the ultimate reform being a "single payer" pool.

Ideally, all Americans should be in the same risk pool—one big group open to all taxpaying residents, with the most purchasing power to negotiate the best rates from medical providers, and offering the least risk for each group member because risk is spread over 350 million people.

The interest groups that represent the medical-insurance complex, particularly the insurance companies, don't want every American in the same pool, though. Neither does the American Medical Association and the Pharmaceutical Research and Manufacturing Association of America. They know that larger groups mean more purchasing power and leverage for patients, and the likelihood of greater scrutiny and regulation of their charges and practices. The pros and "cons" of a single risk pool are summarized in table 9.

The United States has the most costly and least efficient system in the world. The World Health Organization ranks the United States thirty-seventh of 191 countries for "overall health system performance," seventy-second for "level of health," and first for "health expenditures per capita." Moving toward the shared-risk approach is the only way to change these statistics. The simplest way, the public option or a Medicare program that covers every American who wants it, was taken off the table in Washington. But there are fifty more tables in the United States, and more than half of them can be set by the people through the ballot process. The public option should also go back on the table in Washington one day, when a window opens that cannot be closed. Or, inevitably, a state will throw that rock through the window of the Capitol and spark a movement. Until then, though, any alternative that advances the issues must be built on the bedrock of the public's values.

Table 9. Everyone into the Risk Pool: Pro and Con		
Power of the Pool	**Benefits**	**"Fear Factor" Argument against Change**
Bulk purchasing power	The bigger the buyer, the cheaper the price.	Who wants government in our medicine cabinets?
		Choice of drugs and development of new cures will shrink.
Standardized benefits	Security and protection.	Lowest common denominator care. Rationing of medical procedures. "Death panels."
One huge network of doctors and hospitals	Choice and affordability.	Loss of choice and access to best doctors.
Cost controls over doctors, hospitals, and medical providers	Savings mean the health care system can treat more patients.	The best doctors won't practice and hospitals will provide shoddy care.

The Populist Principles behind Reform

The progressive reform effort must stand on solid populist principles that reflect a commonsense understanding of what's gone wrong with health care and health care reform. The following are three key themes around which to organize.

Follow the Money

There is enough money in the system to cover everyone, but it's being mismanaged. No government body is now charged with watching and holding down the overall costs of America's health care system by weeding out waste, fraud, greed, and inefficiency. There is no way to cost-effectively cover everyone without the government ensuring reasonable costs for premiums, doctors' fees, hospital services, and drugs. The degree of regulation may be debated, but the wisdom of efficiencies to lower costs, including accountability to impartial regulators, must be a cornerstone of the new progressive health care overhauls.

There's no denying that the United States has the most costly and least efficient system in the world. Every other national health care system in the world has someone watching the money and a national discussion of how it should reasonably be spent. In America, employers pay health insurers to say "no," because they don't want to have to. When Congress started to discuss the issue of what's reasonable to pay for and not to pay for at the end of life, the cash-rich opponents of change effectively raised the specter of "death panels."

There's no denying, however, that the public intuitively understands the medical-insurance complex's rip-off. Average people are the ones being ripped off. Hospital and medical bills are about as easy to decipher as computer code. Reading the language used in health insurance contracts and evidences of coverage is more like interpreting a dialect from the Georgian Republic. Consumers are intentionally deceived because they would never accept the $120 blanket rental at the hospital if they knew that was what the charge was for. Instead, proprietary codes, called CPT codes, obscure the actual service being charged for. You need to pay seventy dollars to the American Medical Association if you want to get all 7,000 CPT codes and try to decipher your bill today. Transparency in billing and disclosure is very hard to argue against, even in Congress, and it is the way in which every patient can watchdog the medical system. Such a small step as clear itemization of every medical bill in everyday language, breaking the code that prevents us from seeing where our money is going, would make a huge difference in empowering every American with tools to expose and confront the rip-off.

Now, consider that the U.S. taxpayer has just invested almost $20 billion in electronic medical-record technology through the federal stimulus package enacted in 2009. I worked with actor Dennis Quaid, whose newborn infants mistakenly received a massive overdose of a blood thinner at a Los Angeles hospital because of the lack of electronic record keeping, to point out the need for moving away from paper records. Both Dennis and I believe that electronic medical records should do far more than protect the quality of our care; they should also track the costs of each treatment we receive. As Dennis says, when you check out of a hotel you can see your bill on the television screen in simple terms, so why can't you do the same with your hospital bill? The potential for electronic medical records to show Americans the nature of the medical rip-off will be a potent force for political change, perhaps the most powerful, if electronic medical record-keeping technology also becomes a cost-keeping technology. It's a cause the White House needs to take up because to date the executive branch has focused only on regulations to make electronic medical records a quality-control mechanism, not a cost-control tool.

The way to win Americans over to the inevitable logic that a government pool is needed to pay and manage medical providers, in order to bring down costs, is to show them the money and how it's misspent. This will create opportunities to point to cost abuse after cost abuse and make the case from the bottom up for a more rational and moral system. Ultimately the immorality of the rip-off will resonate as much for Americans as any force for systemic and comprehensive reform. That could mean a single-payer system one day, like that of every other industrial nation. Showing Americans the problem is the only road.

The likelihood is that President Obama will both learn from and survive his mistakes. It may take the comfort of a second term before he gets health care right, but the seeds of getting it right are the tools to show Americans the problems with the money in the system. This is the two-trillion-dollar question the president tried to dodge for the sake of expediency, but it's unavoidable.

Barack Obama said during his candidacy that if he were starting from scratch, he would support the full shared-risk model of an open Medicare or single-payer system: "If you're starting from scratch, then a single-payer system would probably make sense. But we've got all these legacy systems in place, and managing the transition, as well as adjusting the culture to a different system, would be difficult to pull off. So we may need a system that's not so disruptive that people feel like suddenly what they've known for most of their lives is thrown by the wayside." In Iowa, Obama added, "So what I believe is we should set up a series of choices. . . . Over time it may be that we end up transitioning to such a system. For now, I just want to make sure every American is covered. . . . I don't want to wait for that perfect system. . . . The one thing you should ask about the candidates though is, who's gonna have the capacity to actually deliver on the change? . . . I believe I've got a better capacity to break the gridlock and attract both Independents and Republicans to work together." Since that didn't work, Obama has only one next move. It's got to be tightening the reins on the medical-insurance complex to make Obamacare work right. When industry fights and squirms, as it always does, those mistakes could give our young president what he needs to make the next big leap. It's up to progressives to make him realize, by carrot or stick, what's right for America now.

Real Accountability for Health Insurers

Polls show few industries are hated more than health insurers. Yet no industry in America is as unaccountable. The reason, as with many injustices in America today, is an errant U.S. Supreme Court decision. Long before the Supremes got involved in rigging presidential elections in *Bush v. Gore,* and guaranteeing corporate supremacy in *Citizens United v. Federal Elections Commission,* the 2010 ruling that undid a six-decade-old ban on direct corporate campaign contributions, the Supreme Court supremely screwed most patients seeking justice against their health insurer.

One hundred and thirty-two million Americans receive health insurance in whole or part through a private-sector employer. In 1987 the Supreme Court ruled in *Pilot Life v. Dedeaux* that if the health insurer screws up a claim for these insured, even if it results in death or catastrophic injury, they are out of luck and cannot recover damages. This is the reason Hilda Sarkysian cannot sue CIGNA over the death of her daughter. Americans who get their health insurance by paying on their own or through the government, as employees or Medicare recipients, can sue for damages, but not the lost class of those who get coverage through a private employer. The ruling hinged on a misreading of an arcane law called the Employee Retirement Income Security Act (ERISA), and it superceded state common law under which Americans generally could take their health insurer to court for bad faith in mishandling claims. The practical efforts have been devastating. Health insurers know that in most cases they won't be accountable, even if their wrongful denial of care kills a patient. So why would insurers ever quickly approve expensive care if there was no financial penalty for denying it? What if a bank robber faced no penalty? This is the dirty little secret of why health insurers today give Americans such a hard time.

That the issue could be totally missing from the discussion of health care reform in 2009 baffled no one more than Hilda Sarkysian. When her daughter died, Hilda soon found that her family had no legal remedy. The high-profile media attention caught the eye of famous criminal attorney Mark Geragos, who handled Michael Jackson's case, among others. He tried to sue CIGNA only to find out the *Pilot Life* ruling wouldn't allow it.

I remember the day I introduced Wendell Potter at one of his first coming-out speeches in San Francisco. Wendell talked about how the Sarkysians' case spurred his change of heart. CIGNA's response to reporting on the speech in the *San Francisco Chronicle* the next morning was that the Sarkysians' case had been dismissed, and CIGNA had been vindicated. In fact, the judge had no choice. The quote made me so angry that I made sure *Dateline NBC* knew about the story, and, indeed, the hour-long show that featured the "When Hilda Met Wendell" moment in January 2010 explained the issue. Geragos found another way to hold CIGNA accountable. At a rally at CIGNA's headquarters in Philadelphia soon after Nataline died, organized by the California Nurses Association, a CIGNA employee watching from the offices gave the finger to Hilda. That allowed Geragos to sue the company for intentional infliction of emotional distress. The irony is that in America you can sue if someone flips you off but not if a health insurer denies your daughter a potentially lifesaving liver transplant.

Democrats recognized the injustice of the *Pilot Life* ruling, and the popular power of the issue, in the late 1990s, and by 2001 they were storming on the floors of Congress against the only industry in America that could not be held accountable in court. On June 19, 2001, Senator Kennedy gave his opening speech to the Senate on a bill that would have allowed patients to hold health insurers financially accountable when they cause harm. He said, "No other industry in America enjoys immunity from accountability for its actions, and the insurance industry does not deserve it either. Few, if any, provisions will do more to guarantee that your HMO does the right thing than the knowledge that it can be sued if it does the wrong thing."

The GOP majority could be blamed for the failure of Kennedy's 2001 legislation. When Democrats had the numerical advantage and drafted their health care plan in 2009, though, they forgot all about the injustice and left the restoration of legal accountability on the cutting-room floor.

It's not hard to see how that happened. The main architect of health care reform, Senate Finance Committee chair Max Baucus, was also the second largest recipient of campaign contributions from the health insurance industry on Capitol Hill. Consumer Watchdog's first major report in Washington, D.C., pointed that fact out early on, yet Baucus stayed in charge of the debate. Even the liberal lions in the Senate and House of Representatives failed to stand on the legal-accountability principles they had espoused eight years earlier under the reasoning that it would burden an already difficult lift. The failure to stand on principle on an issue that is all about morality was part of what doomed comprehensive reform from the start. It should have been about not winning sixty votes in the Senate, but forcing Congress to succumb to what's right and what's popular, like holding health insurers accountable.

Families like the Sarkysians exist in every state and every congressional district. The likes of Max Baucus would be powerless against their stories if the president took up their cause. As long as *Pilot Life* is the law of the land, Americans may have health insurance, but it's very likely they won't be covered when they need it most. Ironically, government officials themselves are not subject to the ruling and have access to the courts. It's yet another hypocrisy of the health care system that is perfect for reminding politicians of in dramatic ways.

Go After the Drug Dealers

On the first anniversary of his presidential election, with his health care plan on the ropes, President Obama sent me, and millions of others on his list, an e-mail and video message. He reminded me of his words on election night: victory alone was not the change we sought, but only the chance for us to make that change. Of course, this time, the president's words sounded hollow, not authentic. His pitch was for me to keep knocking on doors and making phone calls for the cause of change. Like many Americans at the time, I found myself wondering what Obama had done for change lately. I remember first feeling betrayed by the president when I heard in the spring of 2009 about the deal the White House made with the drug companies on health care reform. During the campaign, Obama said he would haul the pharmaceutical executives before Congress and make them answer on C-SPAN about why prescription drug prices in America were 66 percent more than in other countries. It was the populist process that appealed to me, the disinfectant of sunlight sprayed from the presidential pulpit.

Then the media reported that Obama won the drug companies over to health care reform by agreeing not to have the government negotiate cheaper prices through bulk purchasing in Medicare. Obama had abandoned a core campaign pledge. The White House deal was reportedly that in exchange for not pushing the drug makers to give bulk discounts to the government—the same kind Costco, Aetna, and large employers receive—the industry would lay out hundreds of millions of dollars for television advertising on behalf of his health care proposals. The betrayed promise of bulk purchasing of prescription drugs by Medicare and other federal programs hit many of us who understood the potential for huge savings particularly hard. If the nation's prescription drug costs are about 10 percent of health care expenses, then reducing their cost by 66 percent, the savings every other nation in the world receives because it buys in bulk, is the easiest way to cut health care costs by 6 percent without breaking a sweat. Powerful Democratic House of Representatives Commerce Committee chairman Henry Waxman rightly declared he would not abide by the deal and pressed the White House for details. Progressives should not live with it either. After all, why should Americans be the suckers of the world?

Any authentic, genuine reform effort must start with the bipartisan notion of Medicare buying prescription drugs in bulk. The Veterans Administration does it and receives big savings. The drug companies argue research and development will suffer if Americans pay less, and that the most effective drugs will not be developed, but the reality is that more than half of the cost of every prescription drug is marketing costs. That's why the rest of the world pays less for their meds. The principle that "the bigger the buyer the better the price" is as American as apple pie, and any real reform must have this as its centerpiece, not only for the savings, but to signify to the American people that it is real and intuitive.

• • •

The campaign for cheaper, affordable, and universal health care needs to be both *for* a policy and, more importantly, *against* an enemy—in this case, the insurers and drug companies. The Tea Party's goal for the coming years will be to paint government as the enemy of patients. Progressives need to target the avarice of the medical-insurance complex and promote reforms that control its abuses and end its oppression of patients.

CHAPTER SIX

TAMING ARNOLD
A Blueprint for Confronting the Audacity of Phony Change

"11/8/05 ARNOLD FALLS! 11:55 PM"

The note in my Moleskine notebook capped the end of a fierce two-year battle with California's celebrity governor. Arnold Schwarzenegger was elected in the California recall election of September 2003 under the promise of cleaning up government as we know it, driving special interests out of the Capitol, and taking money out of politics. In a preview of the 2008 presidential race, change was Schwarzenegger's mantra. Arnold was going to end business as usual. He made Shermanesque statements that Californians hungry for change ate up like candy at Christmas:

"I will go to Sacramento and I will clean house. I don't have to take money from anybody. I have plenty of money."

"Any of those kinds of real big, powerful special interests, if you take money from them, you owe them something."

"It is inherently suspect for politicians to be taking money from lobbyists while they are spending the people's money."

"Money should not unduly influence politics, [and] influence peddling should stop."

"I want to bring the government back to the people."

After the election, he pulled a complete switch. But for close observers, the evidence that Schwarzenegger would betray the public came early during the campaign that won him his seat. The actor-turned-candidate raised more campaign cash than any politician in California political history. More campaign money, in fact, than any American politician in history until that point except for modern presidential candidates. The total topped $129 million and was raked from the biggest special interests in the state, largely big industries, including $20.5 million from real estate, development, and construction; $13.8 million from the financial, accounting, and investing sectors; $5 million from health care; $4.3 million from oil and energy; $3.7 million from insurance; and $3.3 million from car dealers and the automotive industry. And the favors, of course, started to flow.

Publicly, Schwarzenegger claimed to be Mr. Clean. When pressed by reporters about the contributions he was taking from big business, he contended that the corporations were not special interests. Schwarzenegger claimed that the definition of "special interest" was reserved for labor unions and Native American tribes that did business with the state, not the companies that gave him cash. Most Californians had a different definition, as Arnold learned two years later, but at the time voters bought Team Arnold's marketing.

The irony is that the public could not even get close to the people's governor for his inauguration ceremony, but a private luncheon afterwards financed by the Chamber of Commerce gave some of Arnold's biggest donors face time with their governor. The same day Schwarzenegger froze all pending consumer and environmental regulations. That might explain why Arnold was the first candidate for any constitutional office that the Chamber of Commerce had endorsed in over one hundred years. California had just lived through Enron's shafting during the energy crisis and recalled its previous governor, Gray Davis, for pandering to donors. Now Davis's replacement got elected on one big whopper: that he would run out of Sacramento the very special interests that helped elect him and that he pandered to.

So on inauguration day my consumer group launched the blog ArnoldWatch.org to hold California's new governor accountable to his pledge to clean up special-interest control in Sacramento and to chart the influence of big business over his administration. We a hired a twenty-two-foot moving billboard to circle Schwarzenegger's inauguration—and a Chamber of Commerce–sponsored lunch that followed it—printed with *Webster's* definition of "special interest." It reads, "n. a person or group seeking to influence legislative or government policy to further often narrowly defined interests; especially lobby."

Would Arnold's über-brand be big enough to make the public forget common sense and legitimize the man of the corporations as nothing less than a populist brand?

The California Chamber of Commerce, a friendlier-sounding front group for insurance companies, the oil industry, drug makers, and other corporate Goliaths behind it, has long sought to re-brand its consumer and societal takeaways—including restricted legal rights, fewer workplace protections, and reduced state regulation—as populist, even pro-consumer, by claiming, for example, that their policies would lower the cost of products. Arnold's real threat, as we saw it, was that he could make such mumbo jumbo fly based on the same branding principles that won him the governorship.

Schwarzenegger sold himself as a salesman for California, and he knew his marketing prowess. "I am a salesman by nature," the governor said shortly after taking office. "And now most of my energies will go to selling California [around the world]. If I can sell tickets to my movies like *Red Sonja* and *Last Action Hero*, you know I can sell just about anything." Promoting the most verifiable but least credible promise is the quintessential marketing formula if you're trying to sell something that might not ultimately live up to expectations, and Arnold knew it well. People like "100% satisfaction guaranteed" because it sounds too verifiable to lie about. The equivalent promise in a campaign for governor is "sweeping special interests out of government while making it business-friendly," or "balancing the budget without raising taxes or cutting programs."

As we saw it, Arnold's coming out as governor was not so much an inauguration as the launching of a new super-brand for big business. If the public didn't stop Schwarzenegger, the Chamber would have a new shaman to make their old agenda into a blockbuster. It wouldn't be business as usual in the Capitol, but big business as never before, on steroids.

The only thing to stand in the way of Arnold redefining the corporation's place was the dictionary. So we threw that dictionary at Schwarzenegger for the next two years. Actors may lie for a living, but as governor, Arnold's words would have to ring true.

Arnold Watch worked to make certain that there was some truth in Schwarzenegger's advertising.

Schwarzenegger believed his celebrity, brand, and marketing savvy mattered more than the facts. In the recall election, he turned out to be right. Two years later though, on that November night in 2005, the people of California taught Arnold that truth matters more than fiction. The governor had called a special off-year general election to pass five ballot measures he had championed. They were pure Chamber of Commerce and particularly out of step with the public's priorities. The voters turned him down on every proposition, after a campaign that saw his popularity plummet and that reshaped not only California history but Schwarzenegger himself.

California's Populist Uprising

The story of the populist revolt that felled Schwarzenegger and defeated his five reactionary ballot measures is a case study in how the public can rise up to reclaim politics from the rich and powerful when the right spark is lit. It forms a near perfect model for how to fell a seemingly unstoppable Goliath who lies to the public using basic progressive know-how and populist jujitsu. And its lesson is clear: those billing themselves as agents of change had better deliver, or face the consequences.

As the special election results rolled in on that November 2005 night, I found myself at the Beverly Hilton celebrating over mai tais at Trader Vic's with members of the state nurses union who had worked tirelessly to show the public what Schwarzenegger was really made of.

Nearly a year earlier, Schwarzenegger had made a big mistake, the one that proved later to be the tipping point for the celebrity giant. He called a group of California Nurses Association members protesting a Schwarzenegger speech "special interests" and said he was "kicking their butts." This misstep grew a populist movement and ultimately forced the GOP conservative to become an environment-loving, tax-spending, gay-loving liberal in order to save face with the public.

I had tangled with Arnold Schwarzenegger years before he decided to enter politics. My colleagues and I were taking on "junk faxing," where unwanted fax solicitations tie up your machine and waste your ink. We seized on a federal law to sue junk faxers, and that included a restaurant Arnold Schwarzenegger founded called Schatzi On Main. Our press release noted we were suing "Schwarzenegger's restaurant." But we soon got a long, threatening letter from Schwarzenegger's attorney, Marty Singer, alleging defamation and threatening a lawsuit. Schwarzenegger may have founded the schnitzel shop but no longer owned it. Singer even claimed that disseminating the legal letter itself would be "a violation of the copyright act," since he apparently had copyrighted the communiqué. That was an early clue about how zealously the celebrity guarded his image.

Fast-forward to December 2004. For more than a year, our Arnold Watch project had exposed the contradictions between the Schwarzenegger administration's propaganda and its policies. Here are some of the top gems of Schwarzenegger's "sold out" performance during his first year:

- Drug companies gave $337,200 to Schwarzenegger's campaign committees, more money than to any other American politician except George Bush. Arnold vetoed four popular bills to make prescription drugs cheaper by allowing drug importation and bulk purchasing.
- Nearly $1 million in car-dealer contributions pumped up Schwarzenegger's coffers. Arnold vetoed a greatly stripped-down car-buyers' bill of rights, fired a Department of Motor Vehicles chief hated by the governor's car-dealer donors, and dumped a respected pro-consumer champion at the Bureau of Automotive Repair. It's a pattern that played out elsewhere for other industry donors. Schwarzenegger demanded a freeze on all pending government regulations, a rehash

of every regulation passed during the last five years, the dismissal of pro-consumer regulators, and the appointment of former corporate lobbyists and executives to top posts in his administration. "Oops, I appointed a special interest!" became a regular feature at the blog.

- Big business ponied up the lion's share of the $30 million financing for "The Governator" and his pet causes. After touring the nation on a high-profile campaign to keep jobs from moving out of California, Arnold vetoed legislation to stop big business from shipping California jobs overseas. The apparent motivation: big money from Wal-Mart and others who depend on sweatshop labor. Wal-Mart heir John Walton had given Arnold $200,000 a few weeks before, after Arnold vetoed an increase in the state's minimum wage and a bill to stop Wal-Mart from locking its cleaning and stocking employees inside the store overnight.

- Workers' compensation insurers poured more than $1 million into Team Arnold, including $100,000 on Day 2 of Arnold's administration as he opened up a special session on sky-high workers' compensation premiums. In the end, Schwarzenegger slashed benefits for injured workers but refused to regulate insurance premiums paid by the employer.

- Schwarzenegger fought, and ultimately sued to invalidate, state political practice rules that limited how much his campaign committees could raise. His fund-raising take was twice that of his predecessor, Gray Davis, who lost his seat for being a cash register politician. State laws just wouldn't accommodate Arnold's nearly $100,000 per day habit for his first years in office, so he ultimately got rid of them.

The Arnold Show seemed like another big-budget Hollywood production that forgot what the audience wanted and ignored what the public needed. Still, one year after his recall win, Schwarzenegger's approval ratings were high, and the governor himself seemed to believe he was unstoppable. His arrogance only grew.

We had gotten our message to opinion leaders and investigative journalists, who had started to figure out that Arnold was mostly salesman and little substance. The newspapers were rife with stories of Schwarzenegger's about-face on promises to the public. Schwarzenegger's media team even started to lobby the entertainment press, bypassing what they described as a hostile and negative Sacramento press corps. Arnold's interviews went to *E!*, *Vanity Fair*, and *Entertainment Tonight* rather than the *Los Angeles Times*. The public, though, still held Schwarzenegger in high regard, probably because they tuned out the evening news too.

Most change movements share this characteristic. Opinion leaders are educated about a problem well ahead of the public. These opinion leaders, in this case the media, are the tinder that later lights the wildfire of populism. Connectors, mavens, and vigilantes are the advance guard armed with an information base that lets them spread the news when the opponent of change makes his big mistake, like King George's sixpence tax on tea.

But the public began to pay attention when Schwarzenegger started to call teachers, firefighters, cops, and nurses—working people like you and me—special interests. And then, as they stood up and took more notice, Californians began to figure out that Schwarzenegger called the 2005 special election to do a "Conan the Barbarian" on the working people and their unions. His initiatives tried to:

- take tenure protections from teachers who had opposed the Gov for his education funding cuts;
- curb public-employee unions from giving political contributions without explicit permission from their members—while letting corporations contribute to whomever they pleased without asking shareholders or anyone else;

- give Schwarzenegger dictatorial budget powers to cut education and public safety programs and the teachers, firefighters, cops, and nurses behind them;
- give judges he appointed the power to redraw political lines more to the liking of his Republican party; and
- slash public-employee pensions, although this initiative was withdrawn from the ballot before the vote.

I remember how surreal it felt when I heard the governor's critique of labor unions as "special interests" extend to students and even the disabled. Did this guy really believe his celebrity was big enough to redefine the haves and the have-nots? Then the governor went after one of our closest friends, the California Nurses Association.

California Nurses Fight Back

My consumer group had been shoulder to shoulder with the nurses in the war with HMOs over patients' rights. But it took another battle to stop the hospital industry from recklessly cutting back on the number of registered nurses at the bedside. The situation had grown so dire that nurses reported one patient calling 911 from his hospital bed. Governor Davis finally signed a law guaranteeing a maximum number of patients per nurse in emergency and operating rooms. The first rules took effect just before Schwarzenegger became governor. Then Schwarzenegger raked in $150,000 from hospital giant Kaiser and $1.6 million the health care industry, and he decided to put the next phase of regulations on ice, postponing their further implementation and defending that decision in court. It was the type of naked corruption that provoked movements, and it did.

The California Nurses Association is one of the fastest-growing and most effective unions in America. Led by the fearless and irrepressible Rose Ann DeMoro, the nurses responded to the governor's attack on patient safety by protesting inside the walls of the massive Governors Conference on Women and Families at the

Long Beach convention center. After all, the nursing profession was mostly female, and Arnold had just stepped on their law for a donor that was one of the conference's big corporate sponsors, Kaiser. Schwarzenegger had also faced multiple allegations of inappropriate groping of women aired by the *Los Angeles Times* just before the recall election. And Schwarzenegger's official record for women's rights in Sacramento was a little to the right of Conan the Barbarian's. At the behest of big donors Blue Cross ($142,400) and Health Net ($48,000), the Gov vetoed Senator Jackie Speier's SB 1555 that would have required health insurers to pay for maternity care. Because the guys at the Chamber of Commerce didn't like it, Arnold vetoed Assemblywoman Jenny Oropeza's AB 2317, a bill to strengthen equal-pay-for-equal-work laws. Senator Deborah Ortiz's bill, SB 379, to add new protections for uninsured hospital patients, and Senator Dede Alpert's plan, SB 339, making it easier to collect child support from deadbeats, also got Arnold's manly ax.

The nurses went to Long Beach to pierce the brand, but the mistake they provoked launched a statewide movement. As Schwarzenegger talked before the audience of ten thousand, a small group of nurses interrupted him with chants of protest. As the nurses were escorted out, the governor laughed and told the crowd, "Pay no attention to those voices over there. They are the special interests, and you know what I mean. The special interests don't like me in Sacramento because I am always kicking their butts." It turns out that kicking nurse butt was not popular with Californians.

The conference may have told the stories of incredible women, but Schwarzenegger's comment would be what was remembered. The news coverage at the time was minimal but the remark was on the record and soon on the Internet. A small group of us started having weekly phone calls to fan the exposure and elevate the confrontation.

Director Robert Greenwald and a transplanted East Coast activist he introduced to us, Rick Jacobs, joined with my Consumer Watchdog crew and the nurse leaders to become the nucleus of the campaign that would bring down Schwarzenegger. This was about ten months before the governor's special election. On those initial calls, we decided the way to beat the Hollywood giant was with a simple message: "Nurses, teachers, firefighters, cops, and students are not special interests." Greenwald knew that if the case stayed human, the working people would strike back and beat down the celebrity near-billionaire. Framing guru George Lakoff offered his wisdom along the way.

California initiative wars are some of the most expensive political operations in existence. Obama may have raised $250 million online in one quarter, but one California initiative fight in 2006 over alternative energy sucked up $150 million. Of course, it lost. Schwarzenegger bragged that he would raise $50 million for his 2005 special election ballot initiative campaigns from national sources. Wall Street had the biggest interest in Schwarzenegger's plot to privatize public pension funds, so the investment bankers kicked in with the intent of getting corporate reformers at the state pension plan, CALPERS, off their backs and getting their hands on hundreds of millions of more dollars in 401(k) funds. The governor had essentially put a big For Sale sign on the California ballot initiative process and was marketing himself across America as a celebrity salesman who could peddle snake oil simply by claiming that those against him—a.k.a. non-Schwarzenegger donors—were the "special interests." After his defeat, Schwarzenegger reportedly told Senator Ted Kennedy that he lost because he tried to make the election about him, but his opponents made it all about the issues.

At the time, our little phone klatch knew that we couldn't compete with big money, but that a memorable message and the right messages that got going early would be heard by the bigger moneyed interests against Arnold. We needed to prove it would work, and quickly.

First, Robert Greenwald produced a quick television advertisement using real nurses talking about Schwarzenegger's comment that he was kicking their butt. As Arnold went national with his hands out for money, the nurses went national with a TV advertisement that told America what Schwarzenegger really stands for and whom he stands against. When A&E repeated its bio-pic *Run,*

Arnold, Run about the recall, Americans also saw the sixty-second Greenwald spot. Of course, the Internet site arnoldwatch.net, where you can still view the footage of Arnold's comment juxtaposed with nurses' reactions, propelled that small television advertising buy into a cause. Here's a portion of the video:

> **Arnold Schwarzenegger:** Pay no attention to those voices over there by the way; those are the special interests, if you know what I mean, okay. (Laughs)
>
> **Cindy Nizetich (registered nurse, 15 years):** Politics— to me sometimes it's like you say one thing to get where you need to go and then when you get there, it's like, you don't have to do what you said.
>
> **Jennifer Simmons (registered nurse, 16 years):** He [Arnold] referred to us as a special interest group; yes, that was very insulting.
>
> **Nizetich:** I'm an operating nurse, and I specialize in OBGYN surgery: crashing C-sections, the bleeding, they're very critical. He [Arnold] doesn't deal with what we deal with on a daily basis. He doesn't see what we see.
>
> **Simmons:** Driven by greed and profits . . . which is kind of what they [politicians] do, they really specialize in that kind of stuff, and I think he [Arnold] excels at that.
>
> **Melita Dionosio-Temple (registered nurse, 20 years):** And the one thing that the public should know is one day, you will be in that bed, and realize that because of the number of patients one nurse has to take care of, you may be calling, and there's nobody there.

Taking the Fight to a New Level

We also decided to elevate the confrontation and force more mistakes by getting in Schwarzenegger's face. Everywhere he went, nurses and real people would go. The first stop would be outside Schwarzenegger's house on Super Bowl Sunday, where word had it there was going to be a party. We organized a small crowd of protestors including nurses, students, and consumers who came out on the rainy day to the gates of Arnold's Brentwood estate. Along with the California Nurses Association, we launched the first flight of what we dubbed "Air Arnold." A rent-by-the-hour airplane buzzed the lavish Brentwood neighborhood toting a banner that read: "It's no party for nurses, patients, and students—ArnoldWatch.org"

The plane didn't make many loops before it was grounded by a call from the governor's staff, but the ABC television affiliate caught the action on tape and the news clip played across the state and on the Internet. We also managed to surprise the security guard and march past the gates, only to be turned away up the driveway by California Highway Patrol officers, who called in LAPD reinforcement. But we had made our point. As Schwarzenegger fund-raised across the state and nation, he would have a lot of people's heads turning—up to the sky. He would be followed and exposed. We knew we couldn't compete with Schwarzenegger's brand, but we could puncture it if the messengers and message were right. The first protest was a shot over his bow. Going to someone's house sends a message that the fight is personal.

ArnoldWatch.org was already chronicling every Schwarzenegger fund-raiser invitation we could find. Our tactics for the next nine months were to build a movement that would galvanize all of Arnold's opponents when the time came. The tactics focused on the key elements of any winning populist campaign. They soon grew beyond our little group's control, but the course we set proved solid in the end.

Because this battle had so many elements of a quintessential populist campaign, let's look at some of its core strategies.

Making the Message Bigger Than the Messenger
Schwarzenegger's central strategy was to make his brand bigger than anyone's so that he would have the most credibility with the

public in any fight. The goal of "Air Arnold" was not just to shadow Schwarzenegger, but to fly higher than he was, to get above him metaphorically with some simple truths, populist moral sentiments that no one could deny. Nurses, students, teachers, and working people are not special interests. In another Air Arnold flight over the Capitol dome near a Schwarzenegger fund-raiser, the Air Arnold plane pronounced: "Don't be big business's bully." The Air Arnold flights flew back East, too, at Schwarzenegger fund-raisers. They weren't just media magnets, but a strategy to let Schwarzenegger know our message was bigger than his. The first flight in Schwarzenegger's neighborhood was grounded presumably because it was disturbing the party. That was the point. Message-framing guru George Lakoff wisely advised us that Arnold was seen as big and strong, so showing him as a weakling wouldn't resonate. Instead focusing on his role as a bully could be powerful. Some of the other Air Arnold flights carried that message.

Momentum: Turning 10 into 10,000

Movements must grow. Momentum is everything in political fights. Let it shift or move the other way, and it's easy to go from winning to losing. We may have started out with just a dozen or so demonstrators at the January Super Bowl Sunday party at Schwarzenegger's house, but the numbers grew once television news footage of the event circulated across the state. Other targets of Schwarzenegger's strategy quickly came on board: student groups, labor unions, and senior organizations.

By March, a few thousand protested outside Schwarzenegger's fund-raiser at the Century Plaza hotel in Los Angeles while a small group, including myself, tried to buy our way to the governor's table. The nurses rented a conference room in the hotel, and our small group made its way through the hotel kitchen and service elevators in what felt like a Navy Seal mission. With a video camera rolling, we snuck into the ballroom and occupied a table. A security detail quickly surrounded the table to reject our measly bids for the seats we had taken, which cost the real partygoers $22,300 per seat according to the invitation. I offered 22 cents. The security guards offended a Cedars Sinai nurse by claiming she was contaminating the "endive spears and radicchio cup" salad already set on the table and that the presence of uninvited guests was not "hygienic." That led a Los Angeles firefighter to offer 20 bucks for the menu of "grilled pacific coast halibut in champagne sauce" and "duo chocolate royal time crunch." The room was set for about seven hundred, but only about one hundred high-rollers sipped cocktails as the sit-in crowd was escorted away chanting, "Hey, hey, ho, ho, Arnold's greed has got to go."

Earlier, the Air Arnold banner plane had flown over the fund-raiser with a tip for the Gov: "Arnold: California Is Not for Sale!" The same banner later flew over a reported ten thousand protestors in front of a Schwarzenegger fundraiser at the Ritz Carlton in San Francisco as they swarmed the approaching streets on Nob Hill. Some of Schwarzenegger's guests in limousines had a hard time making their way through the protesting nurses, cops, firefighters, teachers, and working people at the corner of Pine and Grant, including former secretary of state George Schultz.

The television news stories across the state showed the same picture at every fund-raiser: limousines and posh hotels vs. nurses in scrubs, firefighters, cops, and working people. The momentum was with us, and the pictures told voters the story about Schwarzenegger's agenda. Initiative battles in California have become finger-pointing matches, and in the prelude to Schwarzenegger's special election, the sides became clear, particularly when the wealthier unions in the state—the teachers and public employees—spent big bucks to amplify that message on television.

Creating the Wedge: Arnold's Allies Split, Hollywood Speaks Out

One of the sung and unsung heroes of the battle was actor and longtime Democratic activist Warren Beatty. A friend and supporter, Beatty had been instrumental in helping our consumer group establish our annual Rage for Justice Awards dinner a year earlier. In March Beatty accepted our highest honor, the Phillip Burton Public Service Award, and used the stage to unleash a brilliant, blistering critique of Schwarzenegger that was the first by a Hollywood insider. Beatty punctured the celebrity and "bipartisan" bubble Schwarzenegger had inflated around himself by cutting to the core of the governor's hypocrisy. Beatty could speak peer to peer. He had watched as Schwarzenegger had used his platform to belittle Democratic legislators as "girlie men" and "stooges." He now put his celebrity on the line to bring Schwarzenegger down a few notches. This is some of what Beatty said to the four hundred gathered at the Beverly Hills hotel.

> The only taxes the governor has suggested raising are called fees and tuitions that had been provided by the state in programs for people who need help and can least afford to pay. Those programs the governor wants terminated.
>
> At long last, Mr. Terminator, do you want to terminate our decency?
>
> Arnold. Be the action hero I know you can be. Be strong. Stand up and confront the wealthiest 1 percent of Californians who have benefited 12 billion dollars a year from the Bush tax cuts. Business isn't going to leave California. There are too many benefits in being here.
>
> If you're looking for something to terminate—
> Terminate your dinners with the brokers of Wall Street.
> Terminate your dinners with the lobbyists of K Street.
> Terminate collecting out-of-state right-wing money.
>
> Terminate the 70-million-dollar special election you want to hold to divert the public's attention away from the budget.
>
> Postpone your pursuit of the Republican nomination for the presidency. A constitutional amendment will take time. And some day, as the sun rises, the Republican Party will return to the party of Lincoln and Teddy Roosevelt and Eisenhower and Earl Warren and John McCain, and you should start making yourself welcome in it.
>
> Lead. Confront the powerful. . . .

> Not the nurses, not the teachers, or the children, or the students, or the elderly, or the sick, or the cops, or the firemen, or the workers, or the disabled, or the blind, . . . these are not, as you called them, the "special interests." These are people decency demands us to be "especially interested" in.

Beatty gave two more powerful speeches before the special election. This first, though, showed that Schwarzenegger was no Hollywood progressive, which had been a central tenet of his marketing message that he was not a traditional Republican. Days before the special election, Beatty wound up on the front page of the *Los Angeles Times* when he and a busload of nurses, teachers, and other working people tried to hear Schwarzenegger speak at a fundraiser in San Diego. They were turned away by aides who claimed that one had to donate to enter. That mistake drew big media attention across the state right before the election.

Psyching Out the Opponent, Taking Back the Red Carpet

Mind games have always been a part of Schwarzenegger's success. In a profile of the bodybuilder in the *New Yorker*, Connie Bruck quoted weightlifter friend Franco Columbu describing how Schwarzenegger finally beat a nemesis at the Mr. Olympia bodybuilding competition.

> Columbu recalled that in 1969 Schwarzenegger lost the Mr. Olympia competition to Sergio Oliva, a statuesque Cuban bodybuilder known as The Myth. The next year, Columbu continued, Schwarzenegger was determined to vanquish Oliva. Describing that competition, Columbu said, "This shows Arnold's cleverness. He and Sergio were competing, and the judges could not decide between the two of them. They were posing forever. Finally, Arnold turned to Sergio and said, 'Let's go.' Sergio turned around and, without saying goodbye to the audience, he left.

> Arnold took two steps, as though to follow him, but went
> only to the center, and then he turned to the judges, and
> he motioned to the audience like 'He left!' And he started
> posing, posing, posing—and that was it! He did it! Some
> people called it a trick. Sergio was so demoralized, he lost
> every time after that. Arnold won every time."

So, we knew we had to adopt similar strategies to knock him off course. Arnold was used to basking in the public's spotlight, and we knew facing angry fans would be debilitating—that's why we staged the action that kept him from walking the red carpet into the Sacramento premier of a friend's movie; he had to enter from the back, and we had successfully turned Arnold's celebrity around on him. Our message: you can no longer show your face in California if you continue on your course. After the election was over, this type of demoralization would have its greatest impact on Schwarzenegger accepting the error of his ways and embarking on a new course.

None of us knew what Governor Schwarzenegger would do the next day as we waited for the election-night results at the Beverly Hilton in Beverly Hills. The cavernous ballroom had proven a lucky spot for Schwarzenegger to celebrate his political victories in the past. That night, as we walked across the tiered carpet that regularly hosted the Emmys, a defeated tone hung in the air among the news crews assembled to capture Schwarzenegger's surrender. Of the five measures still on the ballot, the polls showed hope for only one or two. Satellite television trucks lined Santa Monica Boulevard to bring the news feed of the the Terminator's terminated initiatives around the world. The nurses had rented out the Trader Vic's private room across the hotel for our "Aloha Arnold" party. It featured a roasted "corporate" pork planted with toothpicks bearing the names of Schwarzenegger's more prominent big business donors. Back in the ballroom there was no food, not even coffee. The navy grogs and mai tais flowed free at the nurses' party, though, and as the final results poured in, almost all the reporters made their way over to Trader Vic's for the pu-pu buffet and open bar. As the precinct numbers of the big-screen television showed Schwarzenegger's initiatives failing across the board, the songs, conga line, and laughter built around the small room. The one hundred or so people in that room knew they had taken down a giant. As one political scientist told the *San Francisco Chronicle*: "You don't win many fights with nurses."

In the end, the nurses had held more than a hundred demonstrations at Schwarzenegger's public appearances. The California Teachers Association and other wealthier unions had broken their bank on television advertisements pointing out the attack on teachers and other public workers. Two days after the loss a contrite Schwarzenegger took the stage at a press conference in Sacramento and said he was wrong.

"If I would do another Terminator movie, I would have the Terminator travel back in time and tell Arnold not to have a special election," he joked. "I should have also listened to my wife, who said to me, 'Don't do this.'"

Populism had proved the weapon in humbling the Goliath star. Schwarzenegger acknowledged his defeat in a stunning political move that saved his career. It sounded to me at the time like a cheating husband asking for a second chance.

"I've always listened very carefully to the people. That's something you have to do in the movie business," Schwarzenegger said. "If one of the movies goes in the toilet, you know it was the wrong story, and that's not the kind of movie you want to do. You then change."

Two hundred and fifty million dollars had been spent on that special election, in addition to the $70 million in taxpayer funds that had been used to stage a statewide election in an "off year" when none was scheduled. What had been settled, more than anything, was Schwarzenegger's definition of special interest and the power of public opinion to tame the rich and powerful. From the moment he ran for governor he pledged the only thing he'd be saying to special interests was "Hasta la vista, baby." After the special election, I don't think I heard, saw, or read about Schwarzenegger uttering the phrase special interests again.

Making Success Pay Off in Future Campaigns

How working people beat Mr. Universe should have been a national example for a labor movement in need of a unified voice. It turned out the real action heroes were the teachers who train, the police who protect, the firefighters who put their lives on the line, and the nurses who care for us. And public opinion is their power. All these groups, and nurses and teachers in particular, got involved in the battle. But in the end, many opinion leaders gave the credit for the win to the teachers' political consultant, Gail Kaufman, who clearly did have the wisdom to stick with the human message our little group of nurses and Consumer Watchdog advocates struck gold with early on. She bought lots and lots of airtime on TV to voice that message—a pricey strategy, but one that also made her a fortune on commissions from the fortune the teachers spent on the advertising buy. The nurses and Consumer Watchdog didn't spend much money on television. We just showed that populist messages and messengers could work, and that putting a lot of people in the streets could still make a difference. So, in the end, the campaign also proved how two conflicting political corollaries are constantly playing out in campaigns for change. First, if you don't care who gets credit, there's no end to what you can accomplish. Second, if you don't get some credit, you won't have the platform to accomplish anything.

What worked and who worked it? Everything and all of us. The political consultants always wind up with the big homes and bigger contracts. For the rest of us, the lessons remain. Public opinion is the most powerful force in the world. Those in public office must stay on the right side of it or risk being run over by the mob.

Ultimately, Arnold won, too. Though the governor suffered a near-knockout blow at the ballot box, his contrition and respect for the public opinion led him to remake himself and regain some of his popularity. He hired Democrats who worked for Gray Davis into his top administrative posts. He led successful efforts to increase the minimum wage and curb greenhouse gas emissions, and he refused to support a ban on gay marriage. Republicans called him traitor, but Californians gave him better grades for a time. Table 10 offers a look at Schwarzenegger's public-approval ratings over time.

Table 10. Trend of Arnold Schwarzenegger's Overall Job Performance as Governor (by percent, among registered voters)			
	Approve	Disapprove	No opinion
July 2010	22%	70%	8%
March 2010	23	71	6
January 2010	27	64	9
October 2009	27	65	8
Late April 2009	33	55	12
March 2009	38	54	8
September 2008	38	52	10
July 2008	40	46	14
May 2008	41	48	11
December 2007	60	31	9
October 2007	56	32	12
August 2007	57	31	12
March 2007	60	29	11
September 2006	48	37	15
July 2006	49	40	11
May 2006	41	46	13
April 2006	39	47	14
February 2006	40	49	11
October 2005	37	56	7
Just Before Special Election			
August 2005	36	52	12
June 2005	37	53	10
February 2005	55	35	10
Call for Special Election			
September 2004	65	22	13
August 2004	65	22	13
May 2004	65	23	12
February 2004	56	26	18
January 2004	52	27	21
Source: Field Poll			

Swaying the New Politician

Schwarzenegger is a master marketer who knows that when one product doesn't sell he needs to find another. Politicians often take the heat for changing their positions, but Schwarzenegger has always seemed to believe that protecting one's brand requires changing one's product to meet the market's expectation. It's a principle often better applied to American business than American politics. But Schwarzenegger, as his term expires in 2010, seems intent on spreading the new paradigm for his so-called post-partisan politician. Schwarzenegger's approval ratings have peaked and dipped based on how well he is in tune with his customers and how he uses his insider connections to present the product they seem to want. Still, at the end of the day, the California public knows what it's been sold and what it actually has. By July 2010, Schwarzenegger's approval rating hit an all-time low. As the *Field Poll* reported, "Schwarzenegger's current 22% approve and 70% disapprove job-performance ratings are equivalent to those given former Governor Gray Davis shortly before he was recalled from office in 2003 and are the lowest job ratings ever given a sitting California Governor in the more than fifty years that the *Field Poll* has been conducting its job assessment measures."

Perhaps President Obama will take note of Schwarzenegger's fate. Arnold Schwarzenegger embodies a new type of politician: one who doesn't just move to the middle but markets the exigency of convenience and candor over principle and endurance. Like it or not, and I don't, this is the new politician. That's why platforms that keep the public cultivating public opinion are so important today.

Schwarzenegger offered this advice for the 2008 presidential candidates before the post–Labor Day sprint to the White House. "Flip-flopping is getting a bad rap, because I think it is great," he said on ABC's *This Week*. "Someone has made a mistake. I mean, someone has, for twenty or thirty years, been in the wrong place with his idea and with his ideology and says, 'You know something? I changed my mind. I am now for this.'"

"As long as he's honest or she's honest, I think that is a wonderful thing. You can change your mind," he said. "I have changed my mind on things, and there is nothing wrong with it."

The power of public opinion is to force a change of heart and mind. Schwarzenegger clearly learned the lesson. Yet the change has to have conviction behind it. There's something disingenuous about a politician who will try to sell anything that he can regardless of his articulated principles. As an actor, Schwarzenegger had the flexibility of enjoying different roles. As a public official, the public needed to believe what he said and did. The art of political possibility inside the Capitol or a statehouse often has led politicians who profess one policy position to embrace another that they say at least moves the issues in the right direction. When is retreat a reversal? When is a compromise really a capitulation? Often it takes advocates who deal with the devil in the details to decipher the language of a compromise so that the public has all the salient facts and can decide for itself. Then the power of public opinion can render its verdict on such "flex-politics."

The battle against Arnold Schwarzenegger proved one important maxim: David doesn't have to fell Goliath; he just has to injure him enough so he comes to his senses and changes direction.

Few presidents should be as sensitive to shifting public opinion as one elected based on a platform of change that average people need. Some of the tactics used against Arnold Schwarzenegger could come in handy against a White House or members of Congress.

In the end, Schwarzenegger and Obama are two sides of the same coin. Both feed on public opinion.

I remember seeing Schwarzenegger work a press line as I stood on the other side just before the 2006 election. He was in front of Los Angeles City Hall with the mayor, former governor Gray Davis, and other polished politicians urging an extension of legislative term limits via ballot measure. I was working the press on the other side of the line, stealing his spotlight for the "no" campaign. In the end, voters sided with us. What struck me was that Schwarzenegger was the only politician to step from behind the microphone and walk right up to the press line, coming across it to meet reporters and answer their questions. He sauntered up, looked into the camera's eye, and gave his best John Wayne delivery. Like most successful celebrities and politicians in America, he fed on the public, more than the issue. It showed to me public opinion could still starve, as well as nourish, not just his agenda, but his persona. And that, in a popular decision maker, is the ultimate lever for creating change.

CHAPTER SEVEN

DIRECT DEMOCRACY
Using the Ballot Measure to Get the Change You Want

A ballot measure forever altered my life. I was twenty-one years old, about to graduate from college, and paying thousands of dollars per year for my auto insurance premiums because of my neighborhood. Along came Proposition 103, which, as I've mentioned earlier, forced auto insurance companies to charge people based on their driving history, not their zip code, and allowed regulators to stop excessive premiums. One of my first votes as an adult was for Proposition 103, and there's nothing like voting for something that changes your own life and stops a practice that you know is wrong. And my first job after college was canvassing door to door in order to raise money to enforce the initiative as insurance companies mounted their legal challenge.

So, for me, the ballot measure has always been a symbol of my power to change things I don't like.

Proposition 103, like most successful ballot measures, was a rare confluence of forces that created a perfect storm. California had enacted mandatory auto insurance two years earlier without requiring premiums be affordable. Rates were rising 11 percent per year when voters were presented with a ballot measure to lower their premiums in November 1988. Harvey Rosenfield and Ralph Nader spent virtually no money and won against a $63.8 million insurance-industry opposition campaign because they spoke through the free media. They boarded a bus that crisscrossed the state to campaign armed with the fairness doctrine, which at the time required television and radio stations to present balanced and equitable coverage of controversial issues of public importance. The insurance companies spent so much on advertising against the proposition that Harvey and Ralph received free air time to balance them out.

One of the reasons Prop 103 prevailed is the insurers spent too much money railing against it, and the public intuitively knew that anything the insurers were backing was the wrong fix. Nader's simple "103 is the one for me" slogan cut through the phalanx of television advertising. The ballot initiative stands as the shining example of how the initiative process can afford average people the opportunity to take on powerful special interests and prevail. Times have changed, but the process still offers great possibility, even if it holds a few more perils.

For all the problems ballot initiative politics present today, the ballot measure offers the best part of modern politics, the ability to directly change injustice, without the main problem with politics today, politicians who are too corrupt or inept to make changes. Fortunately, twenty-four states plus the District of Columbia have a ballot-measure process to circumvent politicians and let citizens write laws themselves.

The power of ballot initiatives is not just that they let citizens write initiatives directly and qualify them with enough signatures of fellow citizens, but that the threat of a ballot measure, or recall or referendum, can force legislators to move or stop them from acting badly. A recall of a politician, where enough signatures force an election to put a sitting politician out of office, can change a state's political direction, as it did in California in 2003 when Californians recalled Democratic governor Gray Davis, largely over his mishandling of the California energy crisis, and then elected Republican Arnold Schwarzenegger to replace him. A referendum gives voters the right to nullify a law passed by the legislature. If enough signatures are submitted within a certain number of days after legislation is enacted, then the public gets to vote on whether they disapprove.

Just mentioning an initiative, with a credible threat of passing it, can change the political dynamics of any issue. For example, no legislature would dare legalize and regulate marijuana, but California voters are taking up that change themselves in November 2010. If legalization passes in California, the movement will soon spread across America, just like many of Proposition 103's insurance reforms did. Initiatives have a way of making issues that are taboo in our culture become completely acceptable.

The fate of the "year of change" election issues—health reform, financial reform, climate change—rests as much in the ballot initiative process as in the U.S. Congress. Americans are likely to have a public option to the private health insurance market only if states make the change themselves via ballot measures. I am currently working in California toward such a ballot initiative in 2012, two years prior to when mandatory health insurance laws take effect. California already enacted a greenhouse gas emissions cap, which has served as a model for national discussion, but it's being challenged at the ballot in November 2010 by oil companies intent on removing themselves from its reach. Initiatives create and end national discussions.

For better or worse, anyone with the will and a little money to play with can engage in ballot-measure politics. The proliferation of special interest initiatives, with fine print that benefits such groups more than the public, has led to a healthy distrust by voters of the process. In California, 60 percent of ballot measures fail because the public is prone to vote no. Still, once in a while, when there is an open window of public sentiment, the right initiative strikes, like Proposition 103, at the right time and changes everything. Those of us who play in the process keep coming back for those moments, or because we are drawn in by our knowledge of the rules of the game to defeat one special interest ploy or another.

Rules of the Ballot Box Road

I have engaged in battle over more than a dozen ballot measures, for and against. There are no hard-and-fast rules, because it's an art, not a science. Those who have thought money is all that it would take have been turned back disappointed because the public still retains the power to decide and cannot be fooled as easily as many interest groups think, or their consultants would have them believe. The rough-and-tumble of the process is also no walk in the park for well-intentioned public servants, who have found out the hard way that the public's distrust and skepticism can be easily fanned by moneyed opponents with an interest in the status quo. I am no master of the process, but I have had the good fortune to win and lose in the system and observe its machinations up close. The following are the basic rules of the road I have learned about ballot-measure politics after two decades of experience.

Start with 70 Percent Approval

Ballot measures are the ultimate weapons of public opinion. Whether you come to the process with or without money, you will need public opinion on your side from the beginning. The less money you have, the stronger the public opinion ratings you need to stand upon. Ballot measures wield public opinion against opponents that don't want to change. Our rule of thumb: begin with 60 to 70 percent approval rating for a ballot measure before you begin because your opponents will knock those numbers down by election day. Wielding public opinion requires you have it in ample supply.

That means the first step in any ballot measure is to test public opinion and hold your ideas for reform up to its lens. If you have the money, a real poll reflecting the composition of likely voters in the state is the most effective way to do it. If you don't, an informal focus group of friends, or a cheap online polling instrument, will at least give you an idea of what type of support you are starting with and baseline arguments that can defeat you. For many progressives, there's a "pollster be damned" tilt, because we want to believe anything is possible. I have learned that it is wise to heed a good pollster's warning. I remember my colleagues and I headed into one very expensive ballot-measure campaign over public financing of elections believing the moment was just right and not needing a pollster to tell us what the public wanted. It was a rude awakening when we learned that voters liked politicians so little that they were unwilling to put up taxpayer funds for their elections, even though cash-register politics was at the heart of their distaste for politicians.

Get the Right Ballot Label; Most of the Time That Is All Voters See

Voters reject most ballot measures because they are naturally, and rightfully, distrustful of the motive of initiative backers. The public knows that special interest groups are the ones with the money to play in the process and are skeptical that ballot initiatives will produce the benefits that they promise to deliver. The first and, in many cases, only impression voters have about a ballot measure is the label that appears on the ballot. The state officials who decide how a ballot label reads have enormous power to help or hurt a ballot measure. The short summary that voters see on the ballot is what they believe, and that's why extensive litigation is fought over ballot descriptions. For low-money or no-money ballot-measure campaigns, the most important asset is a strong ballot label, and what is written in the ballot pamphlet, often called a "title and summary." Ballot measures have often been withdrawn after receiving a bad ballot label.

Put a Cherry on Top

Whatever your initiative is about, it's always nice to throw in something even more popular with the public to sell it and frame it with. Harvey's brainchild in the Prop 103 campaign was a 20 percent rollback of insurance rates—the selling point. And in the end he did deliver $1.43 billion in refunds to consumers. You will need to avoid breaking what's known as the "single subject rule," which requires that an initiative be about only one issue, but it's always nice to throw a sweetener in the mix.

The Weakest Provision Always Sinks an Initiative; Don't Throw in the Kitchen Sink

In an initiative battle, opponents know that finding the Achilles' heel and framing the initiative around its least-liked provision will likely to be enough to stop it. In the battle over Prop 103, insurers didn't talk about the 20 percent premium rollback provision, they attacked the provision ending zip-code-based auto insurance. Insurers knew they could divide rural drivers, who might see premium increases, against urban drivers, who would see decreases in their premiums. Urban Los Angeles went for the initiative in sufficient force to overcome the lost rural counties. There was a great debate during Prop 103's drafting about whether to throw in the ban on zip-code-based auto ratings. In the end, Harvey took the principled position, but it could have cost him the campaign.

Most Initiative Battles Come Down to Finger-Pointing

Ballot measures are instruments of popular anger. Sponsors try to tap into anger about abuses of some kind—in government, markets, the legal system—and opponents try to point out that the initiatives are truly deceptions meant to fool a rightfully angry electorate with a bait-and-switch. Most battles come down to finger-pointing. The details of ballot initiatives are usually way beyond the public's attention span, so what matters in the end is who stands on which side of an issue. Consumer groups versus insurance companies. Cops versus marijuana dispensaries. The governor versus public-employee unions. The public orients itself to initiatives based on who is on what side.

So when beginning an initiative battle it's important to have your sides drawn clearly and to be ready for who will be pointing a finger at whom. Special interest backers of ballot measures like to cloak their presence by putting groups with greater credibility in front of their "coalition." Pulling back the curtain on the true sponsors is sometimes all it takes to stop a ballot measure because the voting public dislikes nothing more than being deceived. In 1996, a coalition of Silicon Valley businessmen, insurers, and Fortunate 500s got together to try to limit the legal rights of California through three ballot initiatives, Propositions 200, 201, and 202, which later became branded by consultant Bill Carrick as "The Terrible 200s." They tried hiding behind a consumer-group front, but a broad public-interest coalition that we organized exposed the corporations that stood behind them. The television advertisements that ran statewide branded the terrible 200s as a weapon of the corporate wolves. Each of the terrible 200s was defeated.

Know Free Media May No Longer Be Enough

Initiative battles have changed during the last decade, just as the traditional media grew less powerful. It's harder and harder to run a successful "free" media campaign in a populous state without paid advertising and win a proposition. This is true particularly when you have moneyed opponents. Prop 103 was the exception to the rule, and the fairness doctrine, since dismantled by the courts and Federal Communications Commission, played a part. Going into battle it's important, when possible, to have allies who can help you be heard through paid advertising on television and radio. The more just your cause, and the better the ballot label, the less you will have to spend on paid advertising. But to win a campaign solely based on "earned media" is the exception rather than the rule in a controversial fight in a state like California.

Even big-money campaigns have difficult odds when there's big money against them. In 2006, Proposition 87, a wellhead tax to be imposed on the state's oil companies had $60 billion in backing mainly from billionaires, led by environmentalist and mega Democratic donor Steve Bing. Bing broke the record for a single individual's spending on a ballot measure with $39 million. The oil companies spent more and beat him. The pro-87 campaign made some key mistakes with its money, including making their paid effort very Democratic, by featuring Bill Clinton in advertising, in a state that increasingly turned independent. However you slice it, you cannot ignore the power of money in initiative battles.

Too much money spent by a single self-interested group, however, can tip the public against a ballot measure. The jujitsu worked in my favor in California's June 2010 primary election when consumer groups defeated two corporate-backed initiatives simply by pointing out the corporate cash behind them. Pacific Gas and Electric spent more than $46 million on Proposition 16 to create a nearly insurmountable two-thirds-vote hurdle before a municipality could create a public utility to challenge the company. Listening to the PG&E advertising, the average voter would think the issue was taxpayer waste, preserving local police departments, and taxpayers' right to vote, not a big utility wanting to stifle competition through a political power play. Opponents had no money to advertise against the measure but launched a "netroots" rebellion on Facebook, Twitter, and e-mail that included authentic homemade videos complaining about PG&E's corruption. Angry PG&E customers in northern California created buzz that reached voters in the south who didn't know much about the utility company's high rates, power shutoffs, and new "smart" meters that seemed to show higher usage. The news media rightly tagged the initiative as a PG&E power grab. State-mandated disclosures at the end of the misleading television advertisements also told voters Pacific Gas and Electric was the sponsor. That was enough for 52 percent of Californians to defeat Prop 16.

Prop 17 on the June 2010 California ballot pitted Consumer Watchdog against our old nemesis Mercury Insurance. Mercury spent $16 million on the initiative to allow it to raise or lower rates based on a factor that voters ruled illegal in 1988 under Prop 103: whether or not you had insurance previously. Courts and regulators had told the company no repeatedly, but hidden behind an industry-sponsored "coalition" of nice-sounding groups, which largely exist only around election time, the insurance company went to voters under the pretense of offering $250 "discounts" for continuous coverage. Thanks to flawless media advocacy by Doug Heller and Harvey Rosenfield every major editorial board in the state weighed in against Proposition 17 on the grounds that it was deceptive, that it would hurt those who didn't drive while in domestic military service, and that it would unfairly raise rates for the unemployed, those least able to afford it. We also raised about $1 million for television advertising to warn the public an insurance company was behind Prop 17. We knew we had to advertise because 17's promise of free money in people's pockets was just too appealing. All we could say in the fifteen-second television ads that we could afford was this: When has an insurance company spent millions of dollars on a ballot measure to save you money? The message was enough to defeat Proposition 17 with 52 percent of the vote. When the voters finally turned our way at 3:00 a.m. on election night, I felt a profound faith in the electorate that had been missing for a few years. We were outspent twelve to one. Consumers were promised $250 each in ubiquitous advertising. The turnout was extraordinarily conservative because the Democratic gubernatorial primary was uncontested. Still, the voters saw through the lie. We won by about 200,000 votes out of the approximately 5 million cast. We broke through with hard work and the right message, crafted by our consultants, *provocateurs extraordinaires* Chris Lehane, Ace Smith, and Lisa Grove, in just the right measure.

If you are going to play in initiative politics, you need to be prepared to raise some money to raise some hell, particularly in expensive media markets like California. It's a daunting task, but with the Internet and social media as potential platforms to raise money, the objective is within greater reach of average people. By contrast, I lost a heartbreaking ballot fight in 2004 when a team of corporations ganged up to take away the public's right to sue for unfair business practices unless there was financial injury. That meant environmental lawsuits and plain old fraud cases went out the door. We fought a great battle in the free media that exposed the culprits, but the momentum turned against us late on the power of their $15 million in paid advertising attacking lawyers. Ignore the power of paid advertising at your own peril. On the other hand, no campaign should only have paid media.

Find a Wedge to Isolate Your Opponents

The successful campaign against the insurer-backed California Proposition 17 in June 2010 sprang in part from the isolation of Mercury Insurance as the only auto insurance company to back the measure. The other insurers decided to stay away from the fight because they feared we would retaliate with a ballot measure that would come at them more directly and take back their profits. USAA, the military insurance company, came out against Proposition 17 early because men and women in the service stationed domestically would be unfairly penalized under the measure. Those who serve us in the military tend to be stationed without their cars and don't need auto insurance. As a result, the Prop 17 plan would have penalized these soldiers, and USAA took umbrage. "Any rating system that does not take into account the unique circumstances military personnel face in maintaining consistent auto insurance does them a disservice and is not acceptable to us," said Michael Mattoch, a veteran and senior legislative counsel for USAA, in the *Los Angeles Times*. That made it far easier to isolate Mercury Insurance as a company that was a pariah in an industry known to be a pariah. The fact that regulators issued a report scolding the company for overcharging consumers for fifteen years just prior to the election also added to the isolation, thanks to Mercury's own greed and mistakes. That created a huge buzz against the company as a rogue power grabber.

These are the forces that work for and against ballot initiatives. They are tricky and don't always bring out the best of the democratic spirit. If you can navigate them, though, you can pass your own laws and stop opponents from taking away rights and privileges that progress has afforded us all. To proceed, there are some basic logistics that vary from state to state. For those who want to build on the new health care law, or create their state's greenhouse gas emission caps, or fill in protections against unfair abuses in the financial system, what follows are the basic steps to set your direct democracy plan in motion.

How to Write and Pass Your Own Ballot Box Law

People writing their own laws for the will of the majority to accept or reject is a noble and ancient tradition. The Greeks let their soldiers vote on battle plans. Massachusetts colonists voted on whether to adopt their own constitution in 1778. In California, populist governor Hiram Johnson gave the public the tools of the ballot initiative in 1911 to combat the grip of the Southern Pacific Railroad over state politics. In modern times, direct democracy has become far more complicated because of the complexity of modern mass communication, but the steps to take to move forward are straightforward. Here's a quick primer on the logistics for writing and passing your own law.

Writing the Measure

Before you begin drafting a ballot measure, you should ideally have public opinion research in your hands about which provisions of your proposal are most likely to be popular with the public. Write it as clearly as possible, with the help of as many friendly lawyers and interested parties from as many different perspectives as possible. The weakest link in the chain, the most innocuous language, could be what your opponents use to defeat the measure. It's always your one mistake that is your biggest problem. The best practice is to have a friendly legislator introduce legislation based on your proposal prior to taking on a ballot measure. You will then have the help of the legislature's lawyers, called legislative counsel, and a legislator's assistants in crafting your language. It's like free legal help and is particularly important in making sure your idea falls in the right code section of the law and does not have unintended consequences. You will also have the benefits of legislative hearings, where your opponents will have to show their faces and throw their best arguments at you. Consider it akin to a dry run on a ballot-measure fight; it will help you fine-tune your proposal before the stakes get high and you start spending any real money. Failure in the legislature is typically the precursor to going to the ballot as well. The public increasingly wants to be presented only with issues the legislature will not move on. The best ammunition to prod a skeptical public to pass a ballot measure is the fact that the legislature refused to act on a similar proposal. It's wise to start one to two years before you intend to go to the ballot in order to get the right words, allies, and money you need to make your effort a success.

Gather Enough Signatures

This step is not for the faint of heart. Every state has different requirements for how many signatures need to be collected to qualify a ballot measure. Bottom line, you will need to look hard at the numbers and deadlines to make sure your approach is realistic. Whether you use volunteer or paid signature gatherers, you'll need to deal with the fact that invalid signatures will drive the number of signatures you need collected up by about 40 percent. In California, more than 700,000 signatures need to be submitted for a ballot measure to qualify, and more than 1 million for a constitutional amendment. You will need allies, those with money and those with genuine volunteer cores, to help you qualify. It's best to have the help of professionals when possible because a small mistake could cost you qualification. For example, the precise text of the initiative will need to be printed on every petition. If the text is off by a single typo, or an earlier version of an initiative is used, the signatures will not be accepted. Such mistakes have cost many a moneyed campaign its prize of qualification. The signature-gathering phase is rife with potential for mistakes. You will need people on your team who have done it before and know how to get it right.

Get the Right Ballot Label

As mentioned above, the short paragraph that appears on the ballot to describe your measure is the best, or worst, bit of advertising a ballot measure can have. The single most important effort any campaign can make is to reach out to the state officials who determine the ballot label as well as the ballot-guide designation, typically called a "title and summary," and educate them about the initiative's true impact, including how it will save the state money and not result in significant state costs. The fiscal impact and friendliness of the ballot label is what will matter most to voters, regardless of the advertising they hear for or against a measure. A great ballot label might even discourage opponents from fighting the proposal with significant resources. Spend as much time and effort to get your research right, and lobby the decision makers early on, because a great ballot label is your best weapon. It's the only thing most voters trust anymore.

Wage the Campaign

This is the fun part. All the tactics discussed in this book have no better forum than a populist ballot-measure campaign to shake things up. Win or lose, in fact, ballot-measure campaigns are essentially public education efforts that raise awareness about critical issues not previously on the radar. Our first HMO patients' rights ballot-measure campaign with the California Nurses Association in 1996 put the issue of patients' rights on the map, but the initiative itself did not succeed.

Initiatives are to be undertaken with caution, but even a loss can be turned into victory if the battle is fought well, and the reason for the defeat is that a big industry or special interest group spent boatloads of money to confuse voters. How you fight and what record you create is everything, and the ballot-measure campaign is a perfect vehicle for the strategies outlined in this guide. Finding a reporter at a major news outlet to be the chronicler of the twists and turns of the initiative campaign, and to blow the whistle on the other side, is key to having a platform to be heard.

Implement the Law

If you do pass your ballot measure, know it's not over, even when it's over. Initially, you will need a legal team in place to stave off those who challenge its legality. Big initial court victories can set the pace and tone. Prop 103's legal defense team quickly defended its rate-freeze provision in court and set up the election of an insurance commissioner and other key provisions of the proposition to proceed quickly. Still, some regulatory and legal battles took years to fight, including the payment of refunds, which totaled about $1.43 billion in the end. Not every initiative has as many working parts, but success against a well-heeled opponent breeds attack on all fronts, most clearly the courts. Over the last two decades, several laws were enacted by the legislature to overturn key pieces of Prop 103, and almost every legislative session there's a bill introduced to do the same. Prop 103 required that legislative amendments "further its purposes" and be passed with a two-thirds majority. As a result courts have thrown out every bill attacking the initiative, though some took years of litigation. It's best to be prepared on the front end with well-vetted language that stands up in court and a legal team ready to fight for the integrity of those words. Prop 103 also specified a private right of action for violation of its provisions, meaning anyone could sue and recover legal fees to protect the law. Twenty years later anger at the legal system and lawyers has grown, but it's probably still worth including a private right of enforcement in any serious reform of an industry even if it can be attacked as opening up the doors to litigation. The provision sends a warning to those who would violate your law and creates a basis to pay the attorneys who will defend the measure.

Corruption of the Initiative Process

A lot has changed since the passage of Prop 103 twenty-two years ago. While important citizen-backed measures have succeeded in California and elsewhere during the last decades, the ballot-measure and referendum process has, as I've mentioned, also been corrupted and dominated by the money of corporate interest groups like oil companies, insurance companies, utilities, and others. Often they are foiled, sometimes they win, but the public's belief in the usefulness of the one arm of government given to them directly has been severely compromised. The easiest way to stop a deceptive ballot measure is to discuss how it is a power grab by a specific interest group, that is, if you can find the platform to speak to the public, which usually involves having to raise money, either from the public or another interest group more aligned with you. Voters are still looking for the real deal and can smell it when they see it. Ballot measures are well worth the time, but they are not to be undertaken without an under-standing of the forces arrayed against the idealistic reformer. I have always found that passionate believers can create their own momen-tum, and the public and those opinion leaders who are the arbiters of the facts will help them in ways that cannot be anticipated. Most state initiative processes are not as daunting as California's, where big money is a factor that cannot be ignored. In the vast majority of states, television and radio advertising may not be necessary to pass a ballot measure, and when necessary, advertising is far more affordable.

The corruption of the initiative process has also spawned reform-ers who claim to want to make the system work better. Among the ideas being considered are allowing the legislature to rewrite faulty ballot measures after qualification, requiring legislative counsel to review ballot measures, and giving the legislature an opportunity to pass a bill before a ballot measure goes before the public. While these efforts are well intentioned, my belief is that the game is the game and changing the rules will undermine one of the purest gifts of direct democracy given to the public. We have stopped more than one dangerous ballot measure because of a drafting or printing error. Our opponents shouldn't be allowed to change their mistakes after submission, because those mistakes reveal their intentions and are the stakes in the fight. If it were hard to slip up and lose the money you put in, how many more special interest groups would venture into the initiative process?

Typically, once signatures are submitted, a proponent cannot withdraw a ballot measure. That's because the proposal belongs to the voters who will vote on the measure. Allowing the legislature to have another crack at the issue, as a way of preventing the voters from having their say, undermines the threat an uncontrollable process holds for special interest groups today. If the legislature, and the industries that fund it, want to concede to reform without a ballot fight, they need to act before signatures are submitted. The power of signatures collected for a ballot measure, which have yet to be turned in, is the ultimate leverage to pass a bill.

That's how my friend Chris Larsen stared down the legislature and won new financial privacy reforms in California. The founder of E-loan and Prosper Marketplace, Chris collected the signatures for a tough financial privacy measure and told the legislature it had a week to pass a strong bill or he would submit the ballot measure. Sure enough, the legislature acted on legislation that had been consistently stalled by the financial lobby. Taking such power away from the people, those who signed the ballot petitions, as well as reformers like Chris Larsen, is not in the interest of a more just and accountable democracy.

The rough-and-tumble of the initiative process, for all its new dependence on big money, still has huge stakes for the establishment, and progressives can use it to shake up those who refuse progress by another means. It's a gift from another progressive age, the Progressive Era of the early twentieth century, when reformers wanted to put a check on the railroad magnates and other robber barons who controlled statehouses across America. The initiative process is the forum where the average person can still take on the rich and powerful and win huge changes for society. It deserves to be preserved and cherished—with all its warts—not undermined.

CHAPTER EIGHT

THE ROAD TO CHEAPER AND CLEANER ENERGY

The worst man-made domestic environmental disaster since the Exxon *Valdez* spill struck on April 20, 2010, when the Deepwater Horizon offshore oil-drilling rig exploded and sank into the Gulf of Mexico. Tens of thousands of barrels of crude oil per day gushed into the Gulf for months, threatening sea life and the economic life of the fishermen, not to mention the fragile ecosystem of the area already torn apart by Hurricane Katrina. BP (formerly British Petroleum), which, ironically, tried to market itself for the half-decade before as "Beyond Petroleum," operated the platform without a detailed disaster plan—the result of BP's intense lobbying to be relieved of that federal requirement. The company also cut corners by not installing a $500,000 remote-control shut-off switch, or backup-blowout preventer, that could have contained the disaster after the rig exploded by sending acoustic signals from off the rig to shut the well down. The spectacle of the seemingly unstoppable oil slick, from the "Drill, Baby, Drill" era, should have immediately lifted the tide for climate reform legislation that lingered on Capitol Hill. The BP spill showed the lunacy of unfettered drilling with oil companies making the rules. It also should have given new legs to Obama's long-standing campaign tenet that we can no longer afford our oil addiction, even though he agreed, as a sop to opponents, to allow even more offshore drilling. Environmentalists urged the White House and allies on the Hill to push for a vote. But the legislation, already larded with handouts to the coal industry and other polluters, still wasn't priced to move.

Despite the horror that unfolded in the Gulf, and the public outrage it stirred, the truth about energy reform often boils down to this: only nosebleed run-ups in gasoline prices get the average person and politician hot and heavy about taking on Big Oil. In America, getting to cleaner energy has to begin with a discussion of cheaper energy. The way to most Americans' hearts is through their wallets, and that's how they learn.

Five-dollar-per-gallon gasoline once seemed unfathomable to most of us. Then came Hurricane Katrina, and its aftermath in the South, when pump prices passed that mark. It was an eye-opener for many Americans, and for politicians who investigated the price gouging. Crude and refinery production in the Gulf had been shut down following the storm. The gasoline in the pumps being sold at $5 per gallon was the same that had been sold for near $2 days before. The gasoline didn't cost any more to make. It was just old-fashioned greed that Republicans and Democrats alike could see through.

In the summer of 2008, I was living in the land of $4.99 gasoline too. The Exxon station's gas-price sign at the corner of Beverly and La Cienega boulevards in Los Angeles, on the border of Beverly Hills, was arguably showing some of the most expensive gas in America at the time. That's why the local ABC television station asked me to do a standup interview in front of it. The only thing I could tell the reporter for sure was that gas prices would come down before the November election. Why would oil companies want a friendly Republican oil man president to face rebellion at the pump just before an election?

My calculation proved to be correct, and gas prices dropped by over $1.50 by Election Day 2008. It wasn't a guess. During the critical 2006 midterm congressional election, when the Democratic Party retook the House of Representatives, the Senate, and a majority of governorships and state legislatures, my consumer group tracked how gasoline prices fell in the run-up to the election as oil companies flooded the market with fuel and took less profit. After Election Day, gasoline prices climbed for months.

If you are an oil executive and you want to keep the Republicans, to whom you give 80 percent of your campaign cash, in control of Congress, what can you do prior to an election? You keep your refineries running at full speed, flood the market with extra fuel, and take less per gallon in profit than usual. The United States Department of Energy data showed that's exactly what the oil companies did in the autumn of 2006. By the second week in October, gasoline prices fell 70 cents from summer's record highs. Refineries were running full throttle and America's gasoline inventories were up nearly 7 percent from the three previous Octobers. Oil companies simply took less profit from their refineries for a short period in 2006 in order to try to influence the political balance of power. Post-election, refineries slowed down, inventories shrank, and gas prices climbed back up. The industry's strategy and our calculations were all confirmed in the quarterly profit reports that came out months after the election.

The point is that oil companies can and do exert control over the price of gasoline. Most Americans believe this and blame oil companies like Exxon for their pain at the pump, particularly as quarterly profit reports continued to prove Exxon's glee at the high price of gasoline. My consumer group's analyses showed that between 2000 and 2008 oil company profits went up in almost direct concert with the price of gasoline.

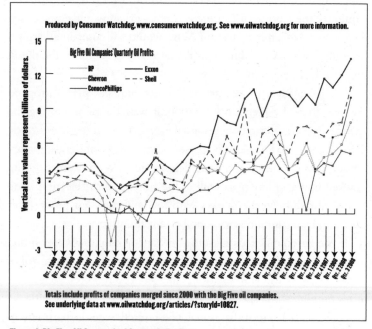

Figure 1. Big Five Oil Companies' Quarterly Profits

Remarkably, the idea that oil companies have control over the price at the pump is controversial in Washington, D.C. Oil company executives point to geopolitical instability, future predictions of crude oil scarcity, OPEC, and other forces beyond their control as the culprits.

The public knows the scoop, and its instincts track the research. Oil companies know they can make more money by making less gasoline, so they do.

I have studied the issue of high gasoline prices for more than a decade. Though I am not crazy about sitting on committees with long investigative hearings, I was tapped in 1999 by then California Assembly speaker Antonio Villaraigosa to represent the Assembly on the California attorney general's task force on gasoline prices. Gas prices were going through the roof, and the speaker wanted a consumer watchdog's eye on the problem.

Here's what I have learned about how the big five oil companies control gasoline prices by making the commodity scarce and keeping the price high. This knowledge is critical to opposing the

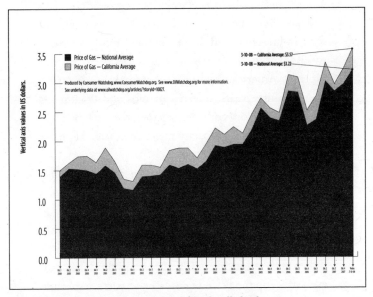

Figure 2. Comparison of Average Gas Prices in California to National

industry's anticonsumer behavior and pushing Americans toward real energy change.

- *Rather than compete with each other to provide more cheaper gasoline, oil companies cheat together to withhold needed gasoline supply from the market.* Consistently, the companies artificially pull back refinery production of gasoline in order to reduce supply coming in during periods of peak demand so they can increase prices. It's legal so long as there is no smoky back room where they talk about it, but they don't need to since industry data about supply flows freely on corporate computer screens. This behavior has been documented by government agencies like the Federal Trade Commission, which found, for example, in an investigation of Midwest gasoline price spikes, that one refiner admitted keeping supply out of a region in need because it would boost prices.
- *Oil companies failed to build ample refining capacity to meet demand.* Over the last twenty years, America's demand for gasoline increased 30 percent and refinery capacity at existing refineries increased only 10 percent. No new American refinery has come on line during the last thirty years. Internal memos and documents from the big oil companies show they deliberately shut down refining capacity in order to have a greater command over the market.
- *The big oil companies have their own crude oil production operations and control substantial foreign production of crude oil.* They profit wildly when the price of crude oil skyrockets, so they have an interest in driving up the price, despite the fact that they blame OPEC for those crude oil increases. The crude oil producers can even drive up the price of crude by restricting gasoline production and trading crude oil among their own

subsidiaries to drive up the price paid for crude by others. Traders with connections to the oil companies can also make big bets on the opaque crude oil futures market to drive up the price and also drive up the value of their Exxon shares.

- *The crude oil that big integrated oil companies use in their own refineries is mostly bought on long-term contracts or through their own production, so the oil companies don't pay the world price for crude oil when it's high.* Their raw material costs are much lower than they would like us to believe. So when the companies raise the price of gasoline in tandem with the run-up in crude oil prices, they are making big profits because Exxon's crude oil unit is charging its own refining unit a higher price for crude than is necessary. The accounting shenanigans result in an overall windfall profit but show the companies' gasoline refineries making little profit, and "upstream" crude-oil production divisions making the lion's share.

Exploiting Tricks of the Oil Trade

My real education with how deceitful oil companies are came when I took on Shell during a big gasoline price spike in the spring of 2004. Shell Oil announced it would be closing its refinery in Bakersfield, which provided 2 percent of California's gasoline at the time and 6 percent of the state's diesel fuel. Reflecting the state of the oil industry, Shell reportedly did not even seek a buyer for the refinery. Wall Street refers to such a closure as "refinery heaven" because it would result in higher prices at Shell's remaining refineries and encourage greater price increases that would benefit every refinery in the market. We started a campaign to get Shell to keep open its seventy-year-old refinery. As I wrote newspaper commentaries and went on radio shows across the state, a whistleblower from Shell found me. He started delivering the internal documents we needed to show the public and politicians that Shell was lying about the reasons for the closure.

The confidential documents we leaked to the media showed that the refinery had the biggest margins, or profit spread, of any Shell refinery in the nation—$23.01 per barrel, about 55 cents profit per gallon. That means, for example, that margins are 36 cents per gallon higher in Bakersfield than in Port Arthur, Texas. The internal document contains a remark under the category of refinery margins: "Wow." Yet Shell kept saying it couldn't put the refinery up for sale because it was not profitable. The company said no other buyer would want the refinery. Shell would make a lot more in profit from the higher price of California gasoline in the long run if the Bakersfield refinery was demolished and gasoline in short supply, than what it would make from the sale.

In fact the whistleblower's documents showed Shell was actually demolishing the refinery, with a timetable for decommissioning and shipping the parts overseas so the refinery could never be reopened. Oil companies consistently complain that environmentalists and "Not in my backyard" communities don't want refineries to open up. Here was an oil company ready to spend tens of millions of dollars to demolish a refinery rather than sell it at a profit.

Experts also came out of the closet to dispute Shell's claim about crude oil availability and show there was enough local crude oil to power the Bakersfield refinery for twenty years. California is ranked third behind Alaska and Texas for size of crude oil reserves and ranks fourth among the states in crude production. Kern County, Bakersfield, is the center of that production.

The evidence we assembled was enough to get two great progressives—Attorney General Bill Lockyer and United States senator Barbara Boxer—involved in grilling Shell about why it would destroy rather than sell the refinery. After enough media, legal, and Congressional pressure, Lockyer and Boxer pushed Shell to sell the refinery to a truck-stop operator, Flying J, though California's attorney general literally had to hire a broker to sell the refinery for Shell.

California's experience shows how much pressure is needed to force oil companies to keep making enough gasoline. It also shows the answer to cheaper fuel is more control over supply. Call it "supply-side" regulation, where the government makes the market achieve the needed supply to meet demand when supply appears to be deliberately shorted. Whether the energy is clean or dirty, more government control is a preventative for wild up-and-down price swings, and such controls have not been even mentioned in the context of the federal energy reforms. There's no question that we need to transition to a petroleum-free future. But in the meantime, we also need to tame the oil companies while the world still runs largely on their product.

Government Oversight: The Missing Link That Progressives Need to Demand

For reform to be successful and progressive, supply-side controls over the clean and dirty energy industries must be a national priority. Price gyrations not only rob family budgets and destabilize the economy, they also cause matching stop-and-start swings in clean-energy investment, preventing steady development of cleaner and cheaper transportation. Regulation of the opaque commodities markets, where the price of crude is often manipulated by those with a vested interest in price run-ups, is also critical for progressive reform.

Incentives for green-collar jobs planted in the financial stimulus bill were the easy pickings for the president. Taking on the oil companies over their prices and climate change is, as Obama might say, a heavy lift. The fact is, Obama has the weight of the world on his back, and he will succeed only by meeting the public on its top priority—high gasoline and energy prices. That means government oversight of supply.

The forces arrayed against supply regulation are significant. It's not just the power of oil companies, but also the preference of the financial establishment that capitalizes them, the tendencies of the environmental movement, and the political culture of the last few decades that stand as significant obstacles. If these forces prevail over the evidence and public opinion, America could well be on its way to an unregulated new bubble in the economy—like the housing and dot-com bubbles before it—as a nation switches gears to an alternative energy economy.

Commoditized energy markets have been the trend in America for the last decade and a half. The belief is they encourage investment in supply. But oil companies like Shell and Exxon control gasoline prices in much the same way that Enron controlled the price of electricity. The company can turn off the flow, make the commodity scarce, and collect huge profits from a scarcer resource.

Energy markets—electricity, natural gas, and petroleum—do work differently from each other, but there is a common theme in many commoditized energy markets—gaming. Oil company consolidation, which has basically left five companies in control of the production and distribution chain, has created a vertical oligopoly. The electricity trading, transmission, and generation system that Enron exploited was supposed to be a highly competitive system. The parallel between Enron and Exxon is important because the future of our energy independence in America is dependent as much on how we regulate all energy markets—including new alternative energy markets—and protect against their gaming, as on what technology we choose to move toward the goal of cheaper and cleaner.

Choosing the wrong technologies, of course, for the sake of political expediency is a very real danger. That's why in the spring of 2010, right before the Gulf disaster, Obama mistakenly embraced offshore drilling as a means to win "bipartisan" support for his energy bill. Clean coal producers, an oxymoron if there ever was one, also fared well under the president's energy reform because the coal-producing states have powerful political representation in the Senate.

One of my colleagues at Consumer Watchdog, Judy Dugan, a longtime journalist, did an impartial look at the options for cleaner, cheaper fuel from the point of view of price, practicality, and environmental impact. Her report card on the developing national cleaner transportation policy delivers some As and Bs, but also some Cs, Ds, and Fs (see table 11). You can bet, though, that Congress

Grade	Technology
Table 11. Report Card for Our Energy Future	
A	Hybrid and plug-in hybrid vehicles, particularly if also capable of using biofuels. Electric vehicles.
B	Ethanol, particularly second-generation cellulosic ethanols.
B	Biodiesel, particularly if produced from a source other than soybeans.
C	Compressed natural gas. (Though the CNG grade improves if it is used only for limited-range trucking and public transit.)
D	Hydrogen. Conventional production methods are energy-wasting; cost and fueling issues are unresolved.
F	Fuel from coal. A polluting pork magnet for coal industry.

will have different priorities based on its political calculus. The job of progressives is to keep our side on track and remind them about what's important.

The Lesson From Enron

My unswerving faith in regulation, with all its bugaboos, as the answer to the "cheaper cleaner" problem stems from my experience as an eyewitness to California's energy crisis as Enron and its unregulated ilk hijacked the state's electricity supply for a huge ransom. The deregulated commodities market they exploited was shaped by the same forces at work in Washington, D.C., trying to exploit the future of America's energy. While the stated goal in each case was "cheaper and cleaner energy," the product was a system rigged for profit for the political players at great cost to the consumer and economy, and no benefit to the environment.

The vulnerability Americans feel each summer to increasingly obscene prices at the pump is the same feeling that struck me back in 2001 during California's electricity crisis. It was almost impossible for me to fathom then how the lights could repeatedly go off in the world's fifth largest and most technologically advanced economy.

There weren't big storms or downed power lines, just good old-fashioned greed. I was at ground zero for the crisis, but at the time few of the people in power believed our consumer group's claims that manipulation by Enron and other profiteering power producers was the culprit. Later, of course, investigations showed Enron had its finger on the switch and was holding Californians' electricity supply hostage for a higher price. The public knew it. If politicians had listened to public opinion, the worst of the crisis would have been avoided. The political landscape of California would have been very different too, without a trace of the conservative Austrian Oak who occupied our governor's office.

Until the winter of 2001, there had been no forced statewide blackouts in California since World War II. By January of that year—three years into a four-year transition to full statewide electricity deregulation—California's so-called utility restructuring law had largely phased out public controls over the wholesale price and supply of electricity. Although only eight months earlier the law was being touted by utilities as a powerful consumer tool, the deregulated electricity system was falling apart.

San Diego, which was the first region to fully deregulate in California, saw electricity rates quadruple during the summer of 2000. Small businesses and restaurants were threatened with closure. Seniors could not afford to turn on their air-conditioning in the heat. However, defying the economic logic proposed to explain these price spikes, the summer demand for electricity was actually lower than in the previous year. The new power producers had no consideration for the societal need to keep seniors cool and small businesses open. They charged whatever the market would bear, not what society needed or deemed reasonable. The situation was so grave that my colleagues and I went to the legislature to demand a temporary rate freeze in the autumn of 2000, which was enacted, though San Diego ratepayers would ultimately be forced to absorb the utility's costs over time.

Our consumer group had entered the deregulation debate two years earlier with an unsuccessful ballot effort to undermine a massive utility company bailout contained in the original deregulation law. In exchange for the public receiving the benefits of a private market, residential and small business ratepayers were required to pay off the utilities' "stranded assets." These were debts from dirty, economically unsound power plants, including nuclear sites, that were bad investments for the utilities. Is it so hard to imagine that in 2010 Exxon would want the same deal for its petroleum-creating assets if it was to be required to invest in cleaner fuels?

By 2001, the $23 billion of bad corporate debt had been paid off by ratepayers. The promised benefits of the private market, however, never materialized. By Christmas of that year, all Californians faced a growing crisis of access and price. The less supply available, the higher the price spiked. The market incentives were precisely for power producers to keep plants off-line, which created artificial shortages that sent the speculative price of electricity sky-high. An unprecedented number of power plants were suddenly shut down for "maintenance problems" at the height of the crisis. Workers at one of these power plants later testified before a state senate committee that equipment to repair the operation was delivered but then disappeared. On some temperate December days the price of energy was more than 3,000 percent the actual costs of producing it. Internal Enron memos released by federal regulators in May 2002 confirmed that California's energy crisis was artificially created by power company manipulation through trading strategies dubbed by Enron "Death Star," "Fat Boy," and "Get Shorty." The Enron memos were written in December 2000 at precisely the moment our consumer group was calling for an end to deregulation—and their strategy was clear:

- Enron created apparent shortages in order to get paid for unnecessary power. According to the memo, "The answer is to artificially increase ('inc') the load [the demand] on the schedule submitted to the ISO [Independent System Operator]." In other words, Enron artificially "congests" the system in order to raise the price of energy.
- Enron created real shortages by temporarily moving power out of state to increase prices. "Such exports may

have contributed to California's Stage 2 Emergency yesterday."

- Enron got paid by the state "a congestion fee" for relieving the artificial congestion it created. "Enron gets paid for moving energy to relieve congestion without actually moving any energy or relieving congestion."
- Enron worked with other power companies to game the system. "Enron's traders have used these nicknames with traders from other companies to identify these strategies."

Remarkably it was an analysis by one of the investment banks, Credit Suisse, that first revealed the smoking gun of California's manufactured energy crisis. It informed its investors in January 2001 that the rolling blackouts plaguing California were simply a negotiating tool, and the California electric grid was not in real trouble. According to the Credit Suisse analyst, "The rolling blackouts in California are more likely to soften up the legislature and the voters to the need for a rate increase than they are indicative of a permanent 'when the lights went out in California' scenario. . . . Relatively soon, some cash infusion to the California public utility system will be accomplished to restore an ongoing flow of power."

California Democratic governor Gray Davis paid the ultimate price for the energy crisis and for ignoring the public's skepticism about the manipulation of the market. Davis refused to take over power plants that were shut down for "maintenance." We had urged him to use his powers of eminent domain to seize the newly unregulated private power plants and force them to provide energy. Instead, Davis was replaced by Arnold Schwarzenegger in a 2003 recall election that turned California politics into a circus. As the popular bumper sticker read: "Black outs in 2001, Gray out in 2003."

Now California has as close to a re-regulated electricity system as possible. Big power consumers cannot buy electricity directly from producers on the free market. Electricity rates are regulated, as is transmission, by the Public Utilities Commission. Generation costs are locked in by long-term contract. Supply and cost are largely controlled by government even as power producers try to convince other state legislatures to take the same leap California did.

Making Choices for a Green Energy Future

The drama that shook California offers some valuable lessons about commoditized energy markets, regardless of how clean the energy they traffic in. The push in Washington, D.C., by banks, venture capitalists, the power industry, and alternative energy producers will be to create incentives for the development of new greener energy choices, but not to have public control over them. That's a recipe for disaster.

The choices America has to make include not only which fuels will replace fossil fuels, but how to develop their generation and transmission. The basis public utilities have traditionally used is "cost plus" pricing. Utilities are told to build wind, solar, or another type of energy plant by a public commission, and the companies are guaranteed the cost of that endeavor plus a fair rate of return set by the commission. The public is guaranteed access to an energy source at a stable price. The utility receives a guaranteed demand for its product and a profit, albeit a reasonable one, usually in the 9 percent or so range.

Venture capitalists and Wall Street banks, however, are likely to argue that if Americans want to bring enough wind farms, solar plants, and other greener energy sources on line, then a big unregulated profit incentive must be waiting at the end of the rainbow. The financiers of the wind farm will want a mega-rate of return, they will argue, to bring enough windmills on line.

The public's conundrum is twofold: how to protect against both supply disruption and price spikes if the next Enron owns the wind farm and/or the transmission system that delivers the energy to the utility or your home. The associations of solar developers, the Solar Energy Industry Association, and wind companies, the American Wind Energy Association, were financial sponsors of the 2008 Democratic National Convention, along with ConocoPhillips and

Texas-based Anadarko Petroleum, one of the world's biggest drilling companies. All the producers are hoping for some governmental help in growing their business. The question, in the case of greener fuels and energy sources, is what the government will require in return for the subsidies or incentives it provides. How regulated will the price and supply be? Will utilities develop the energy under strict government oversight? Will the government develop the transmission systems needed to deliver the new energy to customers, or will private companies control these energy roadways and be allowed to charge huge tolls, as Enron did, to manage the energy traffic? How will the public be guaranteed stable, affordable green energy sources?

Old Texas oil tycoon T. Boone Pickens was one of the first out of the gate with an ambitious plan to make some green off the green energy movement. Nationally he championed wind and solar power, but a 2008 California ballot measure he took on tried to create huge public subsidies for clean-burning hydrogen gas that he had invested in. The billionaire argued he had enough dough and just wanted to save the planet. Proposition 10, however, showed how Pickens's company tried to cash in with the help of the Golden State taxpayer. The measure sought to use taxpayer funds to benefit a specific technology and specific industry that the billionaire controlled: compressed natural gas for motor fuel and producers of such fuel, specifically Pickens. As my colleague Judy Dugan and I wrote to California's legislative analyst for the official ballot summary:

> The measure would in effect transfer California taxpayer funds to the vanity project of a Texas billionaire and intentionally distort natural markets for "clean" vehicles. It would disfavor hybrids and plug-in hybrids, and exclude most biofuels. The measure's unstated but clear goal for the bulk of the taxpayer-paid bond funding is to artificially create a market for natural gas-fueled vehicles to the exclusion of other technology.

California voters saw through Pickens's plot and defeated Prop 10. The fight for progressives in Congress, in statehouses, and at the ballot boxes around the nation will boil down to similar tests. Following are some principles to guide us.

Popular Commandments for Energy Reform

As progressives choose their energy battles, there are some basic tenets that should apply.

Thou Shalt Be Stable and Affordable Above All Else

Whatever choices America makes about substitutes for petroleum and fossil fuels, the guiding principle must be guaranteeing a stable and affordable supply. T. Boone Pickens may own the wind farms, but what price he can charge and how his energy moves to the market, via public or private infrastructure, must be defined before public choices are made about technology investment. Two opposite instincts have driven energy reform in America on issues like gasoline and electricity. The populists have wanted cheaper fuel and cheaper power. The environmentalists have sought cleaner fuel and cleaner energy, and often they have supported higher prices as a way of reducing demand and offering incentives for production. Now there appears to be a common cause. More and more Americans are realizing that "cheaper and cleaner" go together. Average Americans realize that so long as oil companies tightly control petroleum, the companies will always have the nation over a barrel when it comes to price.

Environmentalists are starting to realize that punishing motorists with higher prices leads to anti-environmental proposals to drill for more oil rather than reducing demand appreciably. The main principle to propel green energy forward must be a stable source at a reasonable price. The planning for such a transition must include protections against the type of gaming Enron accomplished. Public-utility-type regulation has proven to deliver the most stable and affordable energy because it entails a legal obligation to provide continuous flow as a necessity of life. Commoditization of energy inevitably leads to huge supply and price swings that plague consumers. If taxpayers or ratepayers are to build the transmission grid to deliver wind, solar, or other green energy to market, they must be guaranteed a continuous supply at a reasonable price. That includes regulating the traditional polluting energy sources needed to fill in the gaps for greener technology like wind power.

The Market Can Offer Carrots, But the Government Must Also Carry a Stick

Supply-side economics, incentives to produce alternative energy, can spur investment in green technologies. But only supply-side regulation can guarantee enough supply of any energy or fuel source, green or not, to meet demand and keep prices low. The Department of Energy already monitors oil refiners and produces a lot of data that has led my consumer group to show market manipulation. Why not grant it emergency powers to force oil companies and other energy producers to make supply meet demand? That includes requiring oil companies to invest their recent world-record profits into making more fuel rather than buying back their stock and pumping up its price, as Exxon has done with tens of billions of dollars per year in profits. The same is true for new investments in green technologies. Green energy is as ripe for market manipulations as the dirty stuff. History has proven that only a government stick can compel energy producers to play fair. For example, tax credits in past federal energy bills for increasing refining capacity—supply-side economics—haven't helped. Without being forced, why would oil companies build new refineries? Any industry that can make more money by making less of a product is going to stay the course. Government regulators need to be the iron hand that evens out the tendencies of energy markets to profit wildly from instability.

Beware of the Banks and Brokers Looking to Build Bubbles

California's electricity crisis and the role of commodities traders in bidding up the price of crude oil to $140 plus per barrel in 2008 prove the same postulate: the hidden hand of Wall Street financiers is more responsible for outrageous costs than any "law" of supply and demand. A very real danger is that the financiers who are look- ing for the next economic bubble and who underwrite both politi- cal parties will dictate the terms of Washington's energy contract with America. As Americans felt profoundly after the collapse of the subprime housing bubble, not to mention the dot-com and Enron bubbles that preceded it, Wall Street's money managers think less about America than the short-term profits on which their bonuses are based. Rational societal decisions shouldn't be made by invest- ment houses that profit from them. Nonetheless, big investments in ethanol, a plant-based substitute for petroleum, were made in part by those who saw synergy between reviving America's automobile industry and developing "energy independence." The ethanol bubble made some venture capitalists a lot of money in the short term. From a long-term policy perspective, though, Detroit produced millions of flex-fuel vehicles that run on ethanol and gasoline, but oil companies never built the gasoline stations to fuel them. In California, a half million flex-fuel vehicles are on the road, but there are only a few dozen public gas stations that offer E-85 fuel for them. In addition, ethanol turned out to be pretty pricey per gallon, as much as gaso- line, owing to crop shortages. Markets know how to make money, but they typically don't deliver on complicated, layered problems like how to integrate flex-fuel vehicles with an E-85 distribution system by oil companies that want to sell petroleum. As a result the early adopters of flex-fuel vehicles don't have much flexibility.

With the balkanized energy systems now in place, and the self- interest by profit-driven companies at each level, only the federal government is equipped to mandate changes that will accommodate the complicated shift to new power and fuel sources.

Thou Shalt Not Greenwash

National energy policy is far too important an endeavor to succumb to the decades-old tactic of the energy companies—giving the public the perception of improving the environment, when in fact there is no appreciable advantage, other than a PR benefit to the sponsor. For example, a carbon-emission trading program, where polluters pay for "credits" based on the amount they pollute, and they can trade the carbon credits as they need more or fewer, may make for a feel-good moment. But if the original carbon credits are priced too low by government, or if large polluters receive "free credits," the system just won't work.

As author Christine MacDonald exposed in her book *Green Inc.*, some of the nation's brand-name environmental groups have excelled at becoming cozy—taking money, board jobs, lucrative contracts, and partnerships—with the largest corporate polluters. And they and their leaders have profited handsomely. The ties are very hard for the public to keep track of, as can be seen in table 12.

Roadblocks to Reform and How to Avoid Them

Many national environmental groups' tendencies will be to accept less than industries can be forced to give under a real national energy policy. Who can the public believe in a debate over energy reform? Progressives must mobilize the public to demand more and hold out for policies that rationally balance the needs of society and the interests of profit. Of course, we will have to overcome the common tricks of the greenwashing trade. Here are some tactics to look out for because they tend to deflate populist momentum for real change.

- *Big PR announcement followed by silence.* Press conferences announcing a consensus for change—in the Rose Garden, a corporate boardroom, or a green pasture surrounded by environmentalists—often don't lead to new policies. Believe in change only when you see it for yourself. Otherwise keep pushing for more than promises and photos. That means realistic timelines, targets, and laws.
- *Loopholes, "opt-outs," and suspension clauses.* Most laws promising big changes come with escape clauses for

Table 12. Corporations and Their Ties to Conservation Groups						
Corporations	CF	CI	ED	TNC	NRDC	WWFUSA
Oil and Gas						
BP	•$	•$	•	•$	•	
ChevronTexaco	•$	•$		•$		
ConocoPhillips	•$	•$	•	•$	•	
ExxonMobil	•$	$		•$		
Shell Oil	•	•$	•	•$	•	
Power						
AES Corp.		•				•
Alliant Energy				•$		
American Electric Power	$			•$		
CONSOL Energy Inc.	•$					
Duke Energy			•	•$	•	
Entergy Corp	•$					

Abbreviations: Conservation Fund (CF); Conservation International (CI); Environmental Defense Fund (ED); The Nature Conservancy (TNC); Natural Resources Defense Council (NRDC); World Wildlife Fund-USA (WWFUSA)

• Indicates partnerships, programs, projects, credit card offerings, membership on boards of directors, joint councils, and advisory boards.
$ Indicates cash donations, cause-related marketing, and other business deals and monetary support.

From *Green, Inc.: An Environmental Insider Reveals How a Good Cause Has Gone Bad*, by Christine MacDonald (Guilford, Conn.: Lyons Press, 2008)

big companies if some portion of their worst fears is being realized.

- *Legislation with targets but no enforcement.* Americans cannot afford to let industries voluntarily develop greener habits. If they were going to do it voluntarily, it would already have happened. Timelines and enforcement procedures are necessary for real change.
- *Announcing a green product long before its production.* Consider the Chevy Volt, which was announced in 2007 with a tsunami of news conferences, bill-

boards, and glossy advertising. It turns out that 2011 will be the first commercial production year for the Volt, which won't arrive in showrooms until the end of 2010. Such hype often diverts populist enthusiasm from more systemic solutions and leads to a false sense of energy security.

- *Punting to a blue-ribbon commission with no power to demand change.* When a company or industry faces a popular mandate to change a practice, it will often avoid new laws by turning over the issue to a blue-ribbon commission that makes recommendations. Those changes are long in coming and rarely do what is promised.

Whatever choices for change the nation now makes, the debate must be driven by sound regulatory principles. That's the one missing link today, and the critical piece of the puzzle public opinion must demand if the public is to be truly on the road to cheaper and cleaner fuel. If Washington fails to deliver on significant energy reform, the answer will come from the states, and from ballot initiatives that citizens can craft to spur and control cleaner, cheaper energy.

CHAPTER NINE

BRINGING WALL STREET BACK UNDER CONTROL

When the second most powerful Democrat in the United States Senate declares that banks "frankly own the place," you can bet real change for Wall Street is not going to come from the inside. Senate majority whip Dick Durbin made the confession to an Illinois radio station, as Wall Street bankers who created the financial crisis fought the Democrats' stronger solutions for staving off another crisis.

By spring 2010, hardly a year after more than $2 trillion in taxpayer bailouts prevented the collapse of the nation's largest banks and brokerages, Wall Street was back to business as usual. The big banks paid out seven-figure bonuses to their executives, raked in billions in profits, and used their political clout on Capitol Hill to stop real regulation of their industry. One in ten Americans was officially unemployed, but with those who had stopped looking for jobs figured in, the real number of citizens out of work was more like one in five. Average people found it hard to access credit, hold on to their homes, and rebuild their devastated savings. Low interest rates meant those on fixed incomes couldn't make ends meet. It's not surprising the public's anger at Wall Street's fabulous fortunes reached epic levels. Inside the Capitol, though, $80 million in campaign contributions from the finance, insurance, and real estate sector held the day. Beating the bankers was no easy trick in a political establishment erected with their campaign cash.

Republicans, egged on by their pollsters, like Frank Luntz, tried to lay the blame at the doorstep of government. Luntz's words to use: "Bureaucrats, wasteful Washington spending, government failures and incompetence, big bank bailout bill, unintended consequences, hardworking taxpayers, another Washington agency, unlimited regulatory powers, red tape."

Democrats, armed with ammo from their own public-opinion prognosticators, like Celinda Lake, made the case for regulation and transparency. Messages that work, according to Lake: "Fairness, transparency, accountability. Critics who offer no solutions and want to continue the same failed polices are doing the bidding of the big banks, Wall Street, and CEOs who want more of the same. We can't leave it up to Wall Street to police themselves. In this country, when you get caught breaking the law, you pay a fine and go to jail. But that doesn't happen if you are a Wall Street fat cat who has given millions in campaign contributions to politicians."

The banking lobby tried to hijack the plans of both parties with claims that government's hands on the problem would only make it worse. Securities and investment firms gave 69 percent of their contributions to Democrats, and commercial banks donated 52 percent of their campaign cash to the majority party too, even as they resisted their reforms.

The public demands were clear enough, even on an issue as confused and muddled as financial reform, where the great excesses of the era sprang from nearly incomprehensible speculation on derivatives and hedges. That confusing information gap made tens of billions of dollars for the schemers, scammers, and Wall Street watchers close enough to know mortgage-backed securities were nothing more than the new junk bonds.

What the Public Wants from Financial Reform

What does the public really desire from and understand about financial reform?

1. *Transparency*. Americans know they don't know enough about the Wall Street bankers who control their money and economy. But they want someone to know and understand what Wall Street is up to. They want transparency about how the system really works and curbs on paying huge bonuses to big brains on Wall Street who made billions simply because they knew how the scams worked. They want to know that the investment bank

advising them to invest in a certain way isn't itself profiting from a bet against that investment. Americans want a balancing of the informational scales between Main Street and Wall Street. They don't want to continue bearing all the risk while bankers reap all the rewards.

2. *No more bailouts.* Americans don't ever again want to bail out a big bank, investment house, or leveraged insurance giant, and they want the bankers to pay a price for taking bailout funds.

3. *A power shift to Main Street.* The public wants to shift the balance of power away from Wall Street. Wall Street's fortunes have grown while Americans' have shrunk, and the American public has taken note. More and more homeowners in over their heads on mortgages are willing to walk away because the zeitgeist has changed to reflect the Wall Street culture. Wall Street bankers got a bailout, so why should average people be stuck with the consequences of their bad investments? Americans don't like this exceptionalism for Wall Street, and they want the rules changed in major ways so that personal responsibility counts again. Accountability needs to be restored for Wall Street if it is to mean anything on Main Street.

Giving the public what it wants on these three issues needs to be the basis for the progressive movement in the coming years. These are the key points progressives need to make repeatedly to do it:

1. George W. Bush created the financial crisis and bailed out his friends on Wall Street, so it's up to us to fix the quagmire he created.

2. If government doesn't exert more control over Wall Street, it will have more control over us.

3. Obama and the Democrats need to be pushed to do much more, but the Tea Party and the GOP have only one plan—do nothing.

Working for the People, Not the Financial Elite

The details of the debate over financial reform may have eluded the American people, but, again, they know a scam when they see it. Hence the people with pitchforks turning up at the Connecticut homes of AIG executives set to reap big bonuses after Uncle Sam saved the company. Unfortunately, President Obama's remedy was to deal with only staving off a future structural collapse of the system, not to satisfy the hunger of the public for the fundamental changes mentioned above.

As progressive pollster Celinda Lake reported to progressive reform groups early in 2010, "Financial reform is a great issue for crystallizing a fight over the economy and establishing who is on the side of working families and Main Street, not Wall Street and CEOs. However, right now voters tend to believe both parties in Washington are helping Wall Street while taxpayers are picking up the tab. Americans rank the president and the Republicans within five points on who is better on the economy (47 percent Obama and 42 percent Republican)—the closest that measure has ever been—and give President Obama negative ratings on the economy (45 percent approve, 53 percent disapprove)."

How Democrats lost the moral high ground on Wall Street regulation is at the heart of the frustration for many of us. Someone in the White House should have one job, reminding the public and press every day that this is Bush's financial crisis and bailout. Instead, Obama's administration has gotten the rap for failing to deal with Wall Street, and progressives feel abandoned in their aspiration for a real leveling of the playing field with the financial establishment.

Republican pollster Luntz told his followers that Americans don't trust government regulation or process to work, and that they should frame the financial reform debate as another "big bank bailout" by government. Luntz writes, "If there is one thing we can all agree on, it's that the bad decisions and harmful policies by Washington bureaucrats that in many ways led to the economic crash must never be repeated." The fact that George W. Bush appointed the do-nothing bureaucrats, like SEC commissioner Chris Cox, and presided over the crash are conveniently forgotten. Of course, the type of "account- ability" Luntz and his followers preach is "government accountabil- ity," which would neuter the effective regulation that Lake's research showed Americans desperately crave. In Lake's poll, two-thirds of Americans support new agencies to protect consumers from bad financial practices, and most think there is too little regulation of Wall Street, credit card companies, and banks. For Luntz's right flank, incompetent government and Washington bureaucrats are the targets.

Understanding Obama's Take on Reform

The key elements of the final Obama overhaul boiled down to:

1. greater government regulation of banks and shadow banks by delegating more power to regulators;
2. new regulation of the opaque and confusing derivatives market, probably the strongest reform on the table;
3. creation of a new Consumer Financial Protection Agency to protect consumers from shady financial prod- ucts, which would offer the most direct help to average Americans; and
4. allowing the government to take over problematic financial institutions to prevent a systemic failure the way they now can take over a bank.

If the goal was to prevent another financial failure, spurred by the opacity of toxic investment, and enflamed by banks and shadow banks calling in debt on each other based on fears they would never be paid, the proposals had a chance to work. They no doubt seemed like sound reasoning and strong medicine from the perspective of the economists who drafted them. Wall Street fought them with an army of 2,100 lobbyists who descended on the Senate in spring 2010, spending $1.4 million per day to weaken stronger proposals the House of Representatives had already passed. The Capitol Hill proposals missed the mark, though, from the point of view of an angry public looking for some equity with Wall Street banks.

The Obama-backed answer to the financial crisis, or at least the one he could pass through Congress, boiled down to making the existing regulators more effective at spotting the "systemic risk" that the financial system itself was unwilling or unable to identify and target. The plan was drafted and sold to the American people by many of the same people at the center of the financial crisis, who had landed within the Obama administration. Treasury secretary Tim Geithner was the head of the New York Fed during the Wall Street meltdown. The government investigation of the AIG bailout laid the blame for pitiful negotiation of bailout terms squarely on his shoulders. Obama's national economic advisor Larry Summers was one of the nation's most arrogant economists, and infamous for his insular ivory-tower thinking. Obama reappointed Federal Reserve chairman Ben Bernanke despite the fact that the banking system tanked on his watch. What kind of message about change did that send to average Americans?

The core of the congressional overhaul was to allow regulators to get together to stop a future "systemic risk" crisis and unwind unsound financial institutions, as well as stopping commercial banks from trading for their own profit with Americans' savings and investment banks from making bets at odds with their clients. So the very regulators who let the crisis happen, including Bernanke, would have more powers to stop what happened on their watch to begin with and would decide how tough future Wall Street rules would be. From the perspective of public opinion, the plan played right into Luntz's public opinion problem for the president. The same Washington bureaucrats who couldn't be trusted would be gaining more power.

The proposals Obama put on the table, minus the consumer protection agency, could have been developed by a McCain administration. They are commonsense proposals that look good on paper to economists who deal in sound economic models. The problem is that when billions in profits are at stake economic models don't work as they should. The Securities and Exchange Commission, for example, fell asleep on the job, yet it would continue to be Wall Street's main regulator under the Obama overhaul. "Regulatory capture," where industries litigate or lobby the effectiveness out of government oversight, is a real problem in virtually every major implementation effort. Incompetence by regulatory agencies is the other major hurdle. The SEC knew about Bernie Madoff's fraud as early as 2000 because a whistleblower named Harry Markopolos documented it for them, but they looked the other way.

Even my progressive allies in the U.S. Senate bailed on Consumer Watchdog years ago when we tried to hold up the nomination of Chris Cox as the SEC chairman. We knew Cox would be a problem because in his former life, prior to joining Congress, he was a defense lawyer for a convicted securities swindler. After leaving the SEC, Cox became a partner with Bingham McCutchen LLP in its corporate, mergers and acquisitions, and securities practice in Orange County, California.

Luntz's public is not mistaken. Regulators are prone to inaction. But great ones have the power to make a big difference too. California insurance commissioner John Garamendi, now a member of Congress, nearly single-handedly took on the insurance industry and delivered tens of billions in savings. We needed to push him sometimes, but he was usually all too eager for the job. That's where progressives can make a real difference in Washington—by watching and pushing the financial policemen Obama assigns to the job under the new overhaul.

His SEC chair Mary Shapiro has done better than her pedigree—as the former head of the financial-industry self-regulating association—would suggest in pushing for some tough reforms, according to Consumer Watchdog's Washington director Carmen Balber. The well-timed SEC prosecution of Goldman Sachs over mortgage securities fraud in April 2010, which allowed the president to demand regulation of derivatives markets as a condition of reform, suggested she could be a strong cop. The crux of the allegations in the case was that a Goldman Sachs executive built a huge toxic-mortgage bond portfolio for investors without telling them that the billionaire who picked the mortgages in the portfolio had bet against them, and the whole scheme was designed to fail. Obama used the Goldman ammunition for this final push. Goldman paid the largest SEC fine ever on the very day financial reform legislation passed the Senate. In his "seal the deal" speech in New York months earlier, Obama declared, "A free market was never meant to be a free license to take whatever you can get, however you can get it." The strong oratory didn't match Americans' expectation of what he would deliver.

The missing element from the Obama plan is a fundamental recognition of what Americans have sacrificed to return the nation to a sounder economic path and what they deserve in return. The biggest remaining bone for consumers in the overhaul is a new consumer-oriented Consumer Financial Protection Bureau. This new place to petition government against financial abuses is something Americans can directly relate to and progressives can target and directly affect the future of.

The Fight Ahead: What Progressives Can Do

Rule making and regulatory enforcement is where some of the greatest progress on issues can be made, but too often that avenue is overlooked by reformers. If structured correctly, the Consumer Financial Protection Bureau (CFPB) will give the public the tools to engage in financial reform. However weak or powerful a new agency is on paper, effective regulation requires the highest degree of transparency, accountability, and public participation. The early months of the agency's implementation will be critical in determining how well it functions in the public interest. The current banking regulators, after all, already have most of the powers that a new consumer agency would have but simply don't use them. Making the agency responsive to the public, not Wall Street, must be a top priority.

The following should be the focus of progressive efforts in the aftermath of the successful financial reform overhaul.

1. *Demand that CFPB appointees and staff be consumer advocates.* The CFPB should be a consumer watchdog, not

an impartial judge of financial matters, and its director and staff must represent that point of view. Every other financial regulator in the federal government serves as an economic mediator. The goal of this agency is explicitly to advocate for consumers, and we must hold it to that standard. This agency should be the balance to the economists, bureaucrats, and lawyers who run federal oversight of Wall Street and are typically co-opted by it. This agency should be the check and balance to all the others, and progressives must demand that.

2. *Call for public participation.* The success of a regulator depends in great part on how much the public is able to oversee its function. Key will be open meetings; the ability of the public to participate in all aspects of agency rule making and administrative proceedings; a citizen fund to reimburse experts for expenses, in order to remove barriers to public participation in the regulatory process; and public-document standards that restrict firms' ability to hide critical information as "proprietary" or otherwise confidential. California has the most effective insurance regulation in America because average citizens can challenge any property-casualty insurance premium increase as excessive. If they, and the actuaries they hire to help them, prove their case, then they win their costs and fees. This system has allowed Consumer Watchdog to stop $1.7 billion in premium hikes between 2003 and 2009 by challenging them through what is known as an "intervener system," and insurers had to pay us for proving them wrong. A similar system should be demanded for the CFPB if it is to attract the highest energy from citizens. Incentives are something Wall Street knows all about, but Main Street should receive them too.

3. *Put consumer advocates back in the White House.* For financial oversight to be truly responsive to public concerns, consumers need a voice not only with regulators, but in the

West Wing too. Prior to the midterm election, progressives should be pushing for the ouster of Larry Summers, White House chief of staff Rahm Emmanuel, and Tim Geithner as a condition of their reengagement. These three men represent the deep ties between Wall Street and Obama, and the president must be put on the spot about their congenital obeisance to the financial industry. In addition, President Obama can and should, without congressional action, appoint the special assistant on consumer affairs in the White House, a post that every Democratic president since John F. Kennedy has filled, except Obama.

He should also re-create the White House Office of Consumer Affairs, which was started under President Nixon. Separate from the Consumer Financial Protection Bureau, this office within the White House can be created with an executive order. There needs to be a consumer voice in the West Wing to balance out the insiders who have been the official voice for the administration on Wall Street. It's an insult to consumers that Obama has sat on his hands on this important post despite a call by consumer groups for it to be filled since his first days in office.

To spur the president, Consumer Watchdog developed an online tool and Facebook application called "Barack and Me." The one-of-a-kind application allowed members of the public to place themselves in a photograph with President Obama, whispering in his ear, and send the photo to the White House with a caption. About five thousand photos have been taken since we put the site up in December 2009. However, despite a positive response from Senate offices and the public, the political showdown around the Consumer Financial Protection Bureau has overshadowed the need for a White House consumer advisor. With the dust settled on the CFPB fight, the air is clear to advance this priority.

4. *Pressure the adminstration to create a real Volcker rule.* The Democratic loss of the Massachusetts Senate seat held by Senator Kennedy emboldened the president to embrace preventing banks from making some speculative investments that are not on behalf of their investors—the so-called Volcker rule, advocated by former Federal Reserve chairman Paul Volcker. The Volcker rule addresses an outrage that is so popular even late-night comedians can talk about it. Investment banks shouldn't be speculating against the interest of their clients. And commercial banks shouldn't be betting their own accounts with taxpayer-insured deposits. The Congressional compromise enacting Obama's overhaul, however, included a watered-down version of the Volcker rule under which banks could still invest billions in proprietary trading, up to a certain threshold. This loophole creates another opportunity for progressives to apply pressure for the correct solution. Implementing the full Volcker rule is an issue that progressives must fight for.

5. *Demand accountability for the opponents of reform.* Financial reform is such a sticky issue with the public that those who stood in its path, regardless of the lack of ambition in the Obama plan, must pay a price in the 2010 midterm election and beyond if the progressive movement is to be able to leverage future votes. Progressives should make it a priority to circulate report cards and scorecards prior to the midterm election that grade elected officials on their votes and their responsiveness to the public on financial reform. The Tea Party can criticize Democrats for a bigger government, but progressives must show the public the cozy relationship between members of Congress and Wall Street bankers. There's nothing to enrage the vital center like a payoff by Wall Street to avoid accountability in Washington.

Here's a simple tactic that has a chance to be effective in every Congressional district in America. "Congressman X took $ ___ in campaign cash from Wall Street and voted against the financial overhaul to regulate Wall Street. Don't let bankers buy your congressional district; vote against Congressman X this fall. Send a message to America that Wall Street shouldn't own Capitol Hill." The Internet tactics mentioned in chapters 3 and 4 offer a full range of options for how to rouse the public with such online messages.

Time for Tough Banking Reforms

The wish list for progressives during the remainder of the president's term has to be an even greater leveling of the power between Wall Street and Main Street. We cannot allow Obama to stop with his initial plans. Wall Street's continued hubris and mistakes will give us opportunities to call for greater change. These are the type of tough reforms we need:

1. *Cap interest rates.* When the capitalist bankers were on the brink of collapse, they suddenly became socialists and sucked up over $2 trillion in government assistance. Instead of then cutting interest rates to the public, as thanks for their rescue, the bankers who took handouts from taxpayers kept charging nosebleed interest to credit card customers. When my colleagues asked for a national interest-rate cap, as part of the federal bailout package, leaders on Capitol Hill would not seriously entertain the notion. They wanted the bailout, and they wanted it without a payout to the public too. Now the Democrats who consummated the Bush bailout are paying the price in the polls. It's time for some commonsense payback for the average taxpayer, whose government bailed out the banks.

Corporations have won exemption from state usury laws by incorporating in Delaware. The federal government should set a national cap on interest rates, a usury law that prohibits Shylock from getting his pound of flesh. This should be a front-and-center issue for progressives, and a key litmus test for every Democratic candidate who wants help being reelected with progressives' backing. What should the interest-rate cap be set at? California's usury law sets unfair interest rates at above 10 percent for nonfinancial institution lenders, or 5 percent above the San Francisco Federal Reserve's lending rate. A national law might have to go higher, but whatever the cap, placing a lid on the price gouging of consumers will show the public and the bankers who is in charge. It's also a policy bankers, conservatives, and Tea Baggers beholden to the GOP operatives will fight tooth and nail. Progressives will have pressure to force many mistakes on an issue of populist dynamite that will detonate the true allegiances of those put on the spot to take a stand.

2. *Restore the walls between commercial banks and investment banks.* Depression-era restraints prohibited a bank holding company from owning other financial institutions. Passed in the wake of the Great Depression in 1933, then repealed in 1999 under President Clinton, the Glass-Steagall Act stood for fiscal responsibility and stability. The removal of the prohibitions spurred the growth of leveraged financial Goliaths like Citigroup that teetered on the abyss during the great financial crisis of 2008 and of banks that grew so large they became "too big to fail."

President Clinton argued in 2008 that repealing the provisions of the Glass-Steagall Act had no impact on the financial crisis but drove the economic prosperity of the previous decade. The fact is that Wall Street's rapaciousness, arrogant egocentrism, opacity, and resistance to the most commonsensical of reforms springs from the consolidation of the financial universe that Clinton's deregulation spurred. Re-regulation via erection of new walls is crucial to taming the Goliaths and putting David back in charge. Wall Street will be making many more mistakes after any marginal financial regulatory advances in 2010. The arrogant always make such mistakes, and one answer for them must be resurrection of the Glass-Steagall walls. This regulation needs to be high on the progressive agenda for a second-term president to restore the trust he's lost. Democratic presidents usually get more progressive in their second terms, but there must be a concerted demand for making this reform for it to have any traction.

3. *Let courts reconsider loan modifications.* President Obama has touted his credit card reform legislation as a major consumer advance of his presidency. A key reform the bankers wouldn't let through was to allow bankruptcy-court judges to modify mortgage rates. Currently judges can change terms of other agreements, but the banking lobby was too strong to allow this critical reform through. That means it's worth fighting for, and progressives need to make sure the president and their other allies do fight for it if they are to have the support we have been asked to give.

4. *Impose a financial transaction and speculation tax.* The theory is that a very small tax on every financial transaction, say ¼ percent, would not hurt average Americans trading in the stock market but would discourage those who buy and sell financial products minute by minute in order to take advantage of the system. Investors invest to spur economic growth and put their money behind endeavors they believe in. Short-term traders are in it for themselves at the expense of the system. They should be deterred and taxed. Wall Street hates nothing more

than a tax, no matter how small, which is yet another reason to make a full-court press for it. The best offense is truly the best defense. The more Wall Street has to defend itself from popular initiatives like these, the less likely it is to come after more from the public.

5. *Limit the size of banks.* The public sentiment from both sides of the aisle is clearly that banks should never be "too big to fail." The obvious populist answer is to make banks smaller. Failed proposals to do so on Capitol Hill would cap the size of a bank's deposits at 10 percent of total deposits, and its non-deposit liabilities at 2 percent of the Gross Domestic Product. The effort to make this change failed on a vote of 33–61 in the U.S. Senate. Democrats voting against the amendment received an average of 55 percent more in campaign contributions from the banking interests affected than Democrats voting for it. Some key liberal thinkers, like Paul Krugman, argue that size matters less than function. Regulation matters more than a limit on mass. It sure is tougher, though, to regulate an institution that cannot be allowed to fail because it is too big. Economists like Krugman may see a rational economic scheme for allowing banks to be of any size, but the public is demanding that there be no repeat of the "too big to fail" bailout. There's only one way. This is a trump card for progressives who want to put all politicians on the hot seat on an issue about which they and conservatives can agree.

CHAPTER TEN

STOPPING THE WARS AND REINVESTING IN AMERICA

Right after President Obama escalated the war in Afghanistan with thirty thousand troops in December 2009, I found myself in the waiting area of Representative Loretta Sanchez's Washington, D.C., office. Her staff explained she would be a few minutes late and pointed me to the television on the wall where C-SPAN was televising the congresswoman in committee disassembling the top-ranking generals in America over Obama's plan.

I was there to talk about not the wars, but health care. Still, when I saw her, I couldn't help but commend her for her cut-to-the-chase advocacy. Sanchez is known by "Loretta" to those of us from Southern California with the good fortune of knowing her as one of the few people in Congress who speaks and votes her conscience regardless of the consequence. She is a true believer, which is truly rare in Washington.

Loretta said it straight: Afghanistan could be the new Vietnam.

Earlier in 2009 Obama sent twenty thousand additional troops with a strategy of disrupting terrorist networks in Afghanistan, building up local security forces, and helping President Karzai create a more effective government. Progressives largely withheld their criticism of the young president. "Now, eight months later, we're being presented the same objectives but being told we need to deploy an additional thirty thousand troops," Loretta said. "I want assurance that these troops are instrumental to achieving our security goals in Afghanistan."

Progressives feared an eight-year war would become an eighty-year war. Thousands had died or become disabled in the Afghanistan and Iraq wars. Hundreds of thousands suffered from post-traumatic stress disorder, depression, or traumatic brain injury. Now Americans were being handed an additional $30-billion price tag for a war approaching $300 billion in taxpayer costs with no end in sight and no exit strategy.

• • •

It is impossible to write a book about getting the change we— as progressives—voted for in the 2008 elections without touching upon Iraq and Afghanistan. Obama heard his supporters say over and over on the campaign trail, "Bring the troops home." No one expected that to be easy. But still, those who felt Bush's wars were unjust wanted them to end, and end rapidly. Hence the surprise when Obama announced that he was committing thirty thousand new troops to Afghanistan and used the occasion of his acceptance of the Nobel Peace Prize to justify the decision in terms that conjured up the image of George W. Bush. "Evil does exist in the world," Obama said in defending the use of force for a "just war." The president argued, much like his predecessor, that "the use of force [is] not only necessary but morally justified" and we "cannot stand idle in the face of threats to the American people."

President Obama claimed he called in the new troops because military leaders said it was necessary. But to antiwar activists, the move was unthinkable. Rather than getting out of wars that have cost us more than $1 trillion to date, at the time of this writing, we were digging ourselves in deeper. Says activist filmmaker Robert Greenwald, "Asking military leaders how many soldiers they need is like asking a five-year-old how much candy he wants."

Greenwald, whose film exposés I've cited throughout this book, has used the screen to protest war as well—through documentaries like *Iraq for Sale: The War Profiteers*. His documentary *Rethink Afghanistan* features experts from Afghanistan, Pakistan, and the United States, explains the war's major issues, and essentially presents what Greenwald considers our flawed strategy in Afghanistan. That documentary was released online, in real time, piece by piece—and for free. The goal was to help build an online, informed antiwar movement. Greenwald teamed with MoveOn to hold hundreds of house parties where the film was screened. Vietnam protesters may have been in the streets and on college campuses, but the antiwar movement that exists today threads through cyberspace and into our living rooms. One of the challenges of that reality is that mainstream media and broad-based public opinion are slower to notice it. But the benefits can be many, too. As we saw in chapters 3 and 4 the Internet can be a powerful tool for change.

Greenwald, like Loretta Sanchez and many others worried about our role there, compares the war in Afghanistan to the war in Vietnam. In fact, Greenwald was re-reading *The Best and the Brightest*, David Halberstam's classic tale of the Vietnam sinkhole, when he was struck by the eerie parallel to the Afghanistan escalation. An administration addicted to action with no perspective on history undertook an invasion without any sense of the American footprint or the moral bankruptcy of its position. The strategic ends in Afghanistan are completely unclear, as they were in Vietnam. As Robert puts it: Al-Qaeda has largely fled Afghanistan, so what are we doing there?

But we are there. And in early June 2010, the war in Afghanistan passed an unfortunate milestone: it became the longest war in U.S. history. That milestone caused Greenwald and the foundation his activist filmmaking spawned—Brave New Foundation—to rally their online community to demand withdrawal from Afghanistan by December 2011. With the Rethink Afghanistan campaign, Greenwald has built an active Facebook community of over thirty thousand, and each Facebook member has an average of 130 friends to whom he or she can forward videos.

Greenwald's is just one of many voices across the nation calling for a clear and quick exit strategy.

What can progressives do to force America out of Afghanistan and bring the troops home?

There are three key questions, right out of Halberstam's history lesson, that progressives need to keep in front of their elected leaders:

1. How many troops?
2. When will we get out?
3. How much is it costing us?

The questions were not asked by elected leaders about Vietnam because of Democrats' fear of looking soft on communism. "Substitute terrorism for communism in 2010 and we have the same old, same old," Greenwald notes.

But the question that has the most leverage for change in this lineup is number 3, and that's where progressives would do well to focus their efforts. The shocking cost of the war given America's dire financial straits is something we must raise at every turn. Because of necessary support and logistics, each individual soldier in Afghanistan costs taxpayers $1 million. So thirty thousand troops comes with a $30-billion price tag. Imagine what kind of education, infrastructure, public works programs, and health care that buys at home.

Conservatives like Glenn Beck are already speaking out about the cost of the war. The fact that the progressive movement has lost ground on the issue of peace to arch-conservatives like Beck shows there's no more important issue to reengage public sentiment. News of the $1 million per soldier figure broke just before Obama sent the extra troops. That he carried on with his plan shows just how tone deaf the president is. Bush's war became Obama's. The National Priorities Project says more than $300 billion has been spent on the Afghanistan war as of June 2010.

Granted there are some things you can't put a price tag on, and proponents of the war have successfully argued to the American public that safety is one of them. But many experts contend that our war in Afghanistan is not making us safer—and that it could be making us far less so by fueling anti-American sentiments and imperiling our economy. I've talked a lot about moral messaging in this book, and putting American soldiers and Afghan citizens in harm's way with little chance of a positive end result raises many moral questions that antiwar activists routinely put to good use. But antiwar campaigns that really want to motivate quick change should relentlessly tally war spending and make it real to the American public.

What's the impact of spending all that money on war?

Greenwald's Brave New Films Web site gives us some measures. One antitank missile in Afghanistan costs $85,000. In California, that could pay a full year of tuition for nine college students. One predator drone in Afghanistan costs $4.5 million. Again, in my state that could fund roughly 840 full Pell grants for college students.

The National Priorities Project has compiled an analysis of the costs of the Afghanistan war on the state and city level. Here are some of the figures that highlight the amount spent on the war in Afghanistan from various cities across the nation:

- $298.3 million in taxes from Tucson, Arizona, enough to provide 5,670 jobs in the health care industry
- $376.7 million in taxes from Oakland, California, equivalent to the salaries of 5,411 elementary school teachers
- $476.5 million in taxes from Orlando, Florida, which would be able to create 8,148 jobs in clean energy

The lost dollars—and the lost opportunities at home—need to be made real to the millions of Americans who are trapped in a bad economy and unable to be effectively buoyed by a government short of funds.

Progressives need to make peace a priority in order to increase domestic spending on students, the unemployed, the national infrastructure, and health care. This will also help progressives reach across the aisle to others who feel similarly. This may be Obama's war, but we cannot afford it, and it's the responsibility of progressives to not allow Glenn Beck to further divide Americans and turn them against their government. A big part of the coming progressive agenda is forcing the president to acknowledge the costs of war are too high and to stick to a hard deadline to pull out of Afghanistan before his second term, which should be a condition of progressives' support for that term. Bush's wars were neither morally nor economically justified. President Obama needs to acknowledge that warmongering is incompatible with the vision he presented to progressives when running for president and become an advocate for peace.

CHAPTER ELEVEN

MAKING YOUR OPINION COUNT

Being heard and felt in this world is never easy, even when there are hundreds of millions of us who feel the same way—even when a presidential election is supposed to be about creating the very change you seek. Asserting our opinions daily may be easier than ever given Internet technology, but making them count is another matter.

In my experience, making our opinions count in daily life, online and off-line, depends as much on good habits as persuasive oratory. Effective advocates possess personal standards and habits that ensure that when they speak they get a response. The skills add up to what one of Consumer Watchdog's supporters, the successful lawyer-philanthropist-businessman Herb Hafif, called "having moves." It occurred to me when he said it, in praise of one of our bigger stunts, that if more like-minded people had more moves, we would have bigger movements.

Change is not the result of one right move, but the consequence of a series of daily decisions we make based on the information we obtain and evaluate to figure out what to do next. Change, by its very nature, is about shaking things up. That's why provoking a reaction is a daily goal of advocacy. While getting the right response is the goal, receiving any response to a series of daily and weekly tasks is what's required to start a dialogue, to receive necessary information, and to evaluate the next move.

After two decades of campaigning for underdogs, in victory and defeat, I have found certain fundamental "moves" work to get a response. Here's my list of the simple day-to-day rituals that make people effective in getting the daily responses and ultimate change they seek at every level.

Write out lists and routinely review them. To-do lists, the simplest idea since the wheel, have the same impact on making change that the wheel has on making transportation. Finding a change maker who doesn't make lists, review them regularly, and stick to them is about as rare as finding a traveler who doesn't believe in the wheel. Of course, making the right list, or ditching the wrong list at the correct time, is the key. But if the list is never made, then the strategy is never set, and the whims of the moment tend to sweep us up into great wastes of time. One of the greatest time-management tips I ever learned is to take time at the end of the day to write the to-do list for the next. That way my vision is clear when I pick up where I left off.

Make sure every phone message you leave is returned and every e-mail accounted for. One of my greatest frustrations is new advocates who tell me they cannot get an answer about an urgent problem because someone has not called them back. Call them again! Call their assistant!! Call their boss!!! Get an answer about why you're not getting an answer, even if you cannot get the answer itself. I learned early in my career, when I was an advocate for the homeless, that minutes count in finding people a roof for the night. I was associate director at a San Pedro, California, homeless shelter. Homeless mothers with children were eligible for public assistance, but we needed to get it for them that day, so they had a voucher for a place to sleep that night. If a welfare worker didn't respond within a certain number of hours we would call the supervisor, then move up the chain of authority to the office of the Los Angeles County director of social services by day's end. There are few workers more fickle than county welfare workers, but they learned to respond in a timely way if they didn't want the director's office calling their boss about a case. Go up the chain of command to get the answer, and it's very likely you will get the call you should have gotten quickly. Be reasonable, but don't tolerate unreasonable response times or else the windows of opportunity to act on information will pass, often as much by design, in order to prevent us from acting, as by accident.

Set deadlines and live by them. Do this for yourself and for others. Deadlines are the only reason newspapers are printed, legislatures act (often not even then), and children go to bed. It seems to be human nature to push up to deadlines to get anything done. I make deadlines for my opponents, allies, and myself. When I myself cannot follow a deadline, I revise it so that I can. Decisions and results require timelines.

Take the HMO patients'-rights fights I have been engaged in. HMOs do not concede anything without consistent and repeated demands. HMOs have time on their side and they know it. They will delay as a tactic of denial. Enough delays will equal a denial for a patient in need of critical care. Because most patients cannot sue HMOs for a denial or delay of treatment and receive damages if they prevail, the companies have an incentive to stonewall because there is no financial penalty. My book *Making a Killing: HMOs and the Threat to Your Health* details patients' travails fighting for medical care they believed they were entitled to under their health insurance policies. Reasonableness always includes a reasonable timetable. When will a decision be made to approve the care? How long will it take to schedule the procedure? HMOs will often fight right up to a deadline, then retreat. A few years ago, for example, my Consumer Watchdog colleague Jerry Flanagan went to the headquarters of Kaiser, the nation's largest HMO, to hold a press conference with the Bennett family, whose three children—two, four, and six years old—suffered from a rare condition known as Sanfilippo syndrome, which is usually fatal by age thirteen. Other insurers provided coverage for the treatment—it costs $600,000 per child—but Kaiser had refused to pay for the stem-cell treatment. When Jerry and the family arrived, they were invited inside. Kaiser officials announced they were approving a $1 million research grant to Duke to pay for the needed procedure. But for the "deadline" of the press conference that decision would likely not have been made.

Put all your demands in writing. Persuasion is the goal of all advocacy. While the spoken word and unspoken messages can tip the balance of power in a campaign, the written word is essential to document the struggle at hand. The right words or action from the right person or people, delivered to the key decision makers at the appropriate time, is the equation for success in advocating any position. Jerry could never have tipped Kaiser's hand with the press conference but for a series of written demands seeking the treatment leading up to it. I have seen the correct "cc" on a letter to an HMO—to a regulator, a credentialing agency, a congressional committee, or me—win patients the right response. Often, decision makers simply need to know they will be accountable to make the right decision. I had a similar experience recently with the case of a sixteen-year-old football hero who was making headway in a specialized care facility after a serious injury to his spine. The HMO wanted to throw him out of the facility and into a nursing home. A consumer reporter from a San Diego television station called me for a phone interview. I told him the governor should intervene to stop the discharge. When the story aired I sent a link to the state's HMO regulator, who called the HMO and told him to let the football hero recover at the facility. The HMO relented.

Writing a thoughtful letter, or creating a simple video record if you can, is the easiest, quickest, and cheapest way to get on the record. Letters create a record of events. Unanswered or unrebutted letters create a record of a different kind, one of indifference. Choose your words carefully, but when you want to make a record, make sure the record is in writing. Remember, often an opponent's big mistake is in how they answer or react to a letter; if they say something unreasonable, that can then be used against them. Failing to answer a serious charge repeatedly can also be a big mistake. When putting it in writing, make sure the writing is good: short, sincere, and salient.

Make sure you do the little things. The biggest mistake that new advocates make is not following through on the little details, be it the phone call that is unreturned, the letter not written at the right time, or taking for granted that someone who told you that they would do something actually did it. The truth is, a lot of the things that look stupid turn out to be really important in the end. Focusing on the little things—the fundamentals—have saved many a campaign. For example, I remember how I recently had to ask a colleague to make a public-records act request to see if she could find some documents about an overseas junket taken by California politicians and the oil industry. She didn't want to go on the fishing expedition and objected on the grounds that surely the media or other watchful eyes would have found such a smoking gun if one existed. I remember telling her that if our history had taught us anything it is that we cannot rely on anyone else to find anything, be it the media, government, or other watchdog groups. She reluctantly made the request and, sure enough, it delivered a mother lode: itineraries and agendas of where top regulators and legislators went as well as what they discussed with Chevron's lobbyist and other top energy companies.

Know when to—and when not to—take credit. This old saying reportedly hung over Ronald Reagan's desk: "There's no limit to what you can accomplish if you don't care who gets credit." It tends to be true, but the adage cuts both ways. You won't be able to keep accomplishing if you don't get credit sometimes for what you genuinely succeed at. The balance of ego and selflessness is important to an effective advocate's success. We build a platform by being known as people who effectively change the balance of power. Yet we could lose power by being seen as people who are not trying to create reasonableness in society but to promote ourselves. The balancing act can be difficult. Generally, take credit when it helps. Give credit when it's due, particularly when there might be negative consequences associated with it.

For example, Arnold Schwarzenegger's fall from power offered a lot of opportunities for Consumer Watchdog and its ArnoldWatch. org to claim we were the first critics and drove the plan that clobbered him. We didn't, because the nurses' union had genuinely been the ground troops in that war, and the teachers had put up big money for television ads that carried our message. So history generally records that the California Nurses Association and California Teachers Association beat the Gov. It's true, and those who were there understand Consumer Watchdog's role. Gray Davis, who remembered our pounding of his role during the energy crisis, approached me after his recall in a parking line following an event honoring California's chief justice a few years back. At the time, ArnoldWatch was alive and well, but Davis had not put two and two together about our role in taking down Schwarzenegger's approval rating. Davis told me that he was dismayed that we had been such a big critic of his but had not gone after Schwarzenegger for similar conflicts of interest. I told the ex-governor about ArnoldWatch.org and asked him to check out the Web site. A few days later I got this e-mail from Davis, always the gentleman: "Without commenting on your criticisms from 1999 to 2003, it is clear you are now doing the Lord's work."

Even more to the point, Schwarzenegger's media aides were frequently complaining to editors and reporters during those years that the press was printing our criticisms verbatim. Often the newspapers didn't quote us at all, because the editors and reporters knew the information stood on its own and didn't want to be open to charges that they were merely reporting information that we released. Davis had obviously heard the drumbeat against Arnold but had not seen our fingerprints on many of those stories. There's quite a bit of gratification in being felt but not seen.

Manage your time and those who would steal it. Don't waste your time or let other people spend it for you. Time is our most precious resource, and too often we get caught up in problems other people should be spending their time on. Don't let meetings run on too long, let people linger needlessly in your office, let callers tie up your phone time. Do block out time for single tasks like writing, make a game of competing with yourself on how quickly you can finish the task, and take time away from your regular routine to get a bird's-eye view of where you are. Make sure the energy put into an e-mail request or organizational commitment is worth the time in terms of the impact.

Let the 80/20 principle ground and guide you. Twenty percent of donors generally provide 80 percent of all money for an organization. Eighty percent of all the work in an organization is done by 20 percent of the people. In business, 80 percent of sales tend to come from 20 percent of customers. The Pareto principle, or 80/20 rule, holds that 80 percent of effects come from 20 percent of the causes. The 80/20 principle tends to work and is a key lens to evaluate whether plans for change are realistic and which people to give your time to. If raising money for a cause, for example, it's most effective to focus on the 20 percent that give 80 percent. If considering allies, find the 20 percent that do 80 percent of the work. Look for the small number of people and groups that do the heavy lifting, and befriend them.

More than a decade ago, Ralph Nader had an idea for a citizens group in California: recruit 1,000 volunteers who each collect 1,000 signatures and $1,000 for citizen-run ballot measures. Nader delivered the idea in a speech in Thousand Oaks, California, where he claimed we needed 1,000 Californians, as strong and sturdy as oak trees, rooted in their community. My consumer group tried to implement the "Oaks Project," only to find that 200 people gathered 80 percent of all the signatures, and it didn't turn out to be enough for statewide qualification. We managed to pass some of the nation's toughest conflict-of-interest laws in four California cities— San Francisco, Pasadena, Claremont, and Santa Monica—based on their efforts. But we learned about the 80/20 principle the hard way. Ralph could hardly believe how much effort we put into that failed model of the Oaks Project. A few years ago I remember reading a proposal for a $6 million plan to build a self-sustaining organization on civil justice from a battery of e-mail solicitations, direct mail, and television ads. The 80/20 rule told me it was too idealistic to ever get off the ground, but the financial donors didn't listen. Sure enough, millions were spent in a matter of months without a lasting trace.

Anticipate incompetence, expect inertia, and count on miscommunication. The e-mail never arrived. Someone else picked up the fax. The reporter was on vacation but forgot to mention that on her voice mail, so her editor didn't see the press release about the announcement until too late in the day. The legislator claims never to have received the memo you sent answering his concerns before the key vote, and that's why he voted the wrong way. Why did we lose? Don't let it be some stupid little thing.

These scenarios keep popping up in my work. Apparently it's okay for the dog to eat the homework in high-stakes politics, when you are not the big campaign contributor. Entropy, in my crude understanding of physics, is the nature of energy systems to run toward chaos and disorganization. The same tends to be true for human organizations and human beings. Entropy almost always sets in right when you expect the most from your allies, particularly when a lot is at stake. People get busy with their own priorities and forget to make or read their own to-do lists. Sometimes there are more sinister motives. Checking in, following up, and anticipating and even expecting the screw-up is the most effective way to keep these type of key misfires from ruining all your work.

Watch for the signs that a well-laid plan is going astray, and don't hesitate to take the pulse and jump in to get things back on track. Your sense of restraint or courtesy may prevent you from making a call or sending an e-mail to check in, but the pushy call is a lot better than the conversation you will have to have about cleaning up a mess that could have been prevented.

Be authentic. Our power lies in being authentic. It's what's missing in politics and what the public wants—wants so badly, in fact, that it will fall for a sense of authenticity above skill, experience, or competence. That may account for why a small-town hockey mom like Sarah Palin could be catapulted with almost no experience into a candidacy for the vice presidency. Authentic voices and messages rise above the fray in politics today. Whenever I have found authentic voices, they have cut through the dizzying indifference of the political spin culture. That's why one patient's HMO nightmare can fell an industry.

Perspective is your only real asset, so nourish it. Find your flow and feed it. "The zone" you probably know best is the same one where Michael Jordan lived when he couldn't miss a jump shot. In my life, it's the place I find, often with music blazing, where I can just keep typing through a tough moment to the other side of a writing assignment. Inspiration may come to me in the early mornings when the house is quiet, and my perspective somehow aligns with my task. Making room for that "flow state," whether it's collecting signatures for an initiative on a hot Sunday afternoon, writing the perfect-pitch e-mail, or making that eye-popping online pamphlet, is the way to bring your energy to trap other people's energy in your cause. Spend time finding the place where it begins. When you get the flow, don't let go, not even to drive to Starbucks. Get whatever is in you out of you first.

It's easier to ask forgiveness than permission, just sometimes more painful later. I have made a career of this tree-house rule. We don't ask companies whether we can release internal documents before we do or they would go to court for an injunction to stop us. Over the years I have learned, though, not to underestimate the pain involved in seeking forgiveness when it's actually required. The forgiveness factor needs to be considered, almost along with the defamation or libel lawsuit, and an accurate record needs to be created. So I have learned to warn politicians and companies, without threatening them, about what's coming if they make the wrong decision. Compulsive letter writing helps show the paper trail of why drastic actions were necessary. It shows that dramatic statements were not capricious but a final resort, in which case neither forgiveness nor permission is warranted.

Matrimony is the only valid excuse for plagiarism. Give credit and praise where it's due; lavish it. Steal your spouse's lines, with her permission of course, but don't take anyone else's without attribution. This mistake has been the downfall of many a gifted writer and leader, one I have never understood. It's like a ticking time bomb that will go off right when you get successful enough that someone is looking for a mistake you might have made.

Know your tendencies and work against them. Science has proven that gut instincts are often the best. Check out Malcolm Gladwell's book *Blink* for the Cliffs Notes version. On the other hand, those who are driven by their passion into a fight often suffer from the same tendency I do: being too reactive. I get pissed off and I want to act. It's a worthwhile emotion, and often worth acting on, but it needs to be tempered with knowledge that the first reaction isn't always the best. Knowing you need to do something soon is far different than doing the first thing that comes to your mind. For a long time

I could not believe I'd actually said the first thing that came out of my mouth until I read it in the next day's newspaper. I remember once really alienating a strong ally on a campaign after an argument about what I perceived as an ill-conceived report. My initial reaction was to say that if the report was issued I would put out a press release condemning it. It did stop the report, but also hurt a key relationship for a long time. Cogitate before you agitate. Just make sure not to miss opportunities.

You cannot be a gadfly if you're worried about being perceived as annoying. Confrontation always runs the risk of making you look unnecessarily aggressive. But if your target is power, confrontation is the only way to get a response, let alone a timely one. I have burned insurance policies at the doorsteps of politicians who wanted to make them worthless, brought dead fishes to hearings to symbolize red-herring proposals, and dumped a truckload of beans on HMO bean counters. If you need to rock the boat, you cannot worry about being soaked by the waves.

Mental sweat is the grease of change. Go to sleep thinking about how to tackle the problem, pace about it, worry. Creating change is an art, and like most art it requires some agonizing about the possibilities and the direction of your energy. Confrontation is supposed to make you uneasy and uncomfortable and embroil you in mental sweat. That's a sign you're on the road to a solution. Of course, watch your tendency to worry, and keep it in check.

Think like a skeptic, act like an optimist. It's easy to be cynical about change in a world that rarely seems to change the way it promises to. Being a skeptic means you are not certain of anything others take for granted. It means you worry doubly over every little issue. So you can identify problems, but you can also take years off your life worrying about ghosts and maybe even mirages. I worry and worry, and sometimes have good cause, including regret. Is it helpful? Ideas sometimes come. Time is sometimes wasted. A lot of human truth is churned in the process. It molds one's being. In the end it is what you do that matters, not necessarily what you think. When you act, take your inner skeptic and inner sweat and turn them into a strong positive statement about the convictions you have arrived at. The outer optimist is what's needed to catalyze change. No one ever followed Woody Allen into battle.

Being lost is part of the journey. How we find our way into the fights of our lives is never a clean and linear path. It's often the diversions, the experiences in the detours, that most define how we see and the moves we make. It's the lessons learned when we get lost on the hike that give us the insight and fortitude to make it to the top of the mountain. Actor Dennis Quaid's detour from Hollywood came when his twin newborn children were given a life-threatening drug overdose at Cedars Sinai hospital in Los Angeles. We worked with Quaid on congressional testimony about the incident. I remember him saying at a meeting that there's a reason things happen to us. For Quaid, his twins' brush with death was forged into an effort to make every hospital in America adopt bar-coding technology, like the scanners in grocery stores, to make sure that other overdoses don't occur.

Show success, not need, to raise money. Being needy may be the biggest mistake those in need of money make. They demonstrate why there is such a great need and how big the problem they want to solve is, which often is perceived by big donors as too big a need to fill. It may be counterintuitive, but more money comes to successful social ventures than ones that are clearly in need of funds. To win dollars you need to project success, not desperation. You need to offer triumph, not neediness. People like to be with those who succeed, not throw their money at problems that may be too big to fix. All fund-raising is about leverage and leaps of faith. Who will step forward first? One donor begets another, and so on. No one likes to be alone. At what point do people believe this is the real thing? When they see that other "successful" people they know are giving, a cause is suddenly perceived as "successful."

Circles that know and help determine change are small and hang together. You need to be invited in. If 20 percent of the people make most of the contributions, an even smaller percentage of that group, who are the most successful contributors, seem to find a way of circling together at the same dinner tables. And it's not just about money, but about people who affect politics in other ways. That's how I got into Ralph Nader's circle relatively quickly as a consumer advocate in the mid-1990s. I made a few key moves that got noticed, like nailing U.S. senator Dianne Feinstein down on a key consumer vote, and suddenly Harvey Rosenfield put me on conference calls with Ralph. Ralph introduced us both to Warren Beatty, who connected us with some people he no doubt wished he had not over the years. Ultimately the buzz precedes you and you run into people who know who you are. When it comes to big money, though, guys like Harvey and me have a hard time breaking into the circles that can write the big checks. Warren may like us, but that doesn't mean we get invited to lunch with his billionaire friends. Money and power run in circles. You need to be invited into them and then buzz around, but there's always a limit to your access if you don't give big money, too.

"Peer to peer" is the way around strangers' fear. I learned this lesson in my first job out of college, knocking on doors for contributions to help enforce insurance reform and Proposition 103. "Your neighbors are fighting back with checks of $35 or more," I would say. Then I would hand over a clipboard of information on top of which was a sheet signed by local donors. Neighbors do what their neighbors do. After I had the first few signatures of neighborhood contributors, I could invoke their names and addresses to generate money at an exponential clip. Peer-to-peer fund-raising, or learning of any kind, is always the most effective. But for that lesson, or that job, I probably would not have taken the path I have.

When you are stuck, walk away, then come back. My friend, mentor, and publisher Jeremy Tarcher taught me this trick. He told me once when I was stuck on a previous book that sometimes we are standing too close to a mural to see the whole thing. He told me to walk away and write about something else for while. The walking away— be it from a bad spot with a politician or my six-year-old son—is always harder than it sounds. But I almost always see the full picture on the way back.

Hope Is Worth Fighting For

Finally, a few last words about fear and change. In my experience, fear is typically what crushes change in society and in people. People are often too afraid to lose what they have in order to get what they need. Things usually don't turn out as well as we want or as badly as we fear. We generally don't take as big a hit for being wrong as we expect, or receive as much credit for being right. The politicians we hate are rarely as bad as we anticipate, and the great ones are rarely as exceptional.

In the middle of the night we may wake up worrying about what's coming next. By morning, we usually realize the dark hours distorted our perspective and perception. Fear is worth fighting against. Hope is worth fighting for, because when it pays off there's a huge ripple, an exponent we could not expect or anticipate, a momentum shift that has a life of its own.

In truth, the only change we can really believe in is the change in ourselves. It's worth taking a gamble on the rest, if for no other reason than what it inspires in us is beyond our power alone. No one knows for sure when we will pass a tipping point for change in society, culture, government, or economics. Who breaks through to whom and when is a mystery until the very end of most struggles. It could be you, or me, who shows up at the right time and place to change history. That's not worth missing for anything. The only thing greater than seeing the world change for the better is knowing we were part of it.

NOTES

Introduction

xi **"Now make me do it."**   The exchange is attributed to a conversation between FDR and civil rights and labor leader A. Phillip Randolph, and Eleanor Roosevelt is said to have said the same phrase to Harry Belafonte. Paul Rogat Loeb, *Soul of a Citizen: Living with Conviction in Challenging Times* (New York: St Martin's Press, 2010), p. 300. Progressive radio host Amy Goodman claimed on her *Democracy Now!* show on January 9, 2009, "I was just speaking with someone who was at a Montclair fund-raising party for Barack Obama a year and a half ago. And he quoted this famous quote from A. Philip Randolph, when he went to FDR to demand something, and FDR turned to him and said, 'Make me do it.'" Interview with Adam Cohen, http://www.democracynow.org/2009/1/9/nothing_to_fear_adam_cohen_on.

xvi **The ballot-initiative process in twenty-four states and the District of Columbia**   The Ballot Initiative Strategy Center at www.ballot.org lists the states and qualification procedures in each one.

Chapter 1: The Art of Change

1 **HMO reforms in forty-four states**   While HMO reforms vary state by state, the test of a strong system for these purposes is whether patients can turn to a panel of independent doctors to overturn a denial of medical care by HMO bureaucrats. Forty-four states have such laws.

3 **luxury junket Speaker Núñez and his wife had taken to South America**   The trip, funded by the Chevron-backed foundation the California Foundation on Energy and the Environmen,t drew widespread media coverage and criticism. For example, Bill Ainsworth, "Special Interests Skirt Gift Limits, Critics Say," *San Diego Union Tribune,* April 6, 2006, http://legacy.signonsandiego.com/news/politics/20070406-9999-1n6trips.html; Consumer Watchdog, formerly called the Foundation for Taxpayer and Consumer Rights, filed a public-records act request with the Public Utilities Commission that uncovered details of the trip, including the agenda and presence of the Chevron executive who attended.

3 **fifty grand in political contributions from Chevron**   Press release, Foundation for Taxpayer and Consumer Rights (now Consumer Watchdog)/Oil Watchdog, "Assembly Speaker's Promised Action to Curb Gasoline Price Spikes Fails as Chevron Money Flows, Says Letter," August

23, 2007, http://www.oilwatchdog.org/articles/?storyId=6743. Also, read the letter in the link, dated August 16, 2007, to Núñez discussing legislation. The legislation in question, mentioned in the letter, included the weakening of refinery-oversight legislation AB 1610, and orphaning of AB 1552, refinery data-reporting legislation. In 2006, Núñez stopped a full assembly vote on a price-gouging law, and 200 in 2007 he created a bill to derail progress on "hot fuel" that halted regulators' approval for temperature-adjusted gasoline, which would have moved the issue forward without legislative intervention. Chevron sent $50,000 to the Democratic party based on fund-raising by the speaker and another $100,000 to the term-limit ballot measure

5 **undermined one of our modest health-insurer reform bills**   The patients' rights bill would have stopped junk health insurance policies that place no out-of-pocket limit on how much insured patients can be charged. Patients and consumer groups urged Núñez, who voted for the bill, to use his leadership post to rally votes for AB 2281 (Chan), as he had for AT&T's telecommunications deregulation bill. Dana Christensen, who was left with $450,000 in medical bills after her husband died from cancer despite being insured, sent a letter to Núñez. Blue Cross asked the speaker to stay out of the fight. Núñez did. And two weeks later, according to state campaign-finance reports, Blue Cross contributed $50,000 to Núñez's ballot-measure committee, enough for two tickets to the World Cup. Núñez never replied to Christensen. More on the fight at http://www.consumerwatchdog.org/politicians/articles/?storyId=788.

5 **AT&T coughed up six figures to sponsor the "Speaker's Cup"**   See *San Francisco Chronicle* blog, "Democrat Lawmakers, Donors Link Up at Pebble Beach," http://www.sfgate.com/cgi-bin/blogs/nov05election/detail?blogid=14&entry_id=4719, and more on the deregulation scheme in my *San Francisco Chronicle* op-ed, "Bad Deal for Cable Customers, AT&T and Assembly Dems Bill's Big Winners," June 25, 2006.

6 **"We don't regulate the health insurance industry"**   Author's transcription of Assembly Health Committee testimony, hearing on Assembly Bill x11, November 14, 2007

6 **the governor reversed his earlier stance**   Schwarzenegger was a vocal proponent of term limits, but he endorsed Prop 93, the term-limits extension, the week of January 18, 2007.

6 **the *Los Angeles Times* printed a report**   Nancy Vogel, "Campaign Cash Gives Nunez Rich Travel Style," *Los Angeles Times*, October 5, 2007.

7 **infamous television clip of the speaker being chased** This KABC-TV clip played statewide: http://www.youtube.com/user/ consumerwatchdog#p/search/1/8Nn31GCpGoc.

7 **$11 million trying to keep Núñez in office** California Secretary of State, http://cal-access.sos.ca.gov/Campaign/Measures/Detail. aspx?id=1299177&session=2007.

7 **"Because of the fact I am a Mexican,"** Jim Sanders, "Nunez Charges Racial Bias in Spending Attack," *Sacramento Bee*, May 22, 2008, recounting interview on Univision's *Voz y Voto* program.

8 **the *Today* show** video at http://www.youtube.com/watch?v=P h6KluqMGQQ&feature=PlayList&p=B453460F6BDAF351&playn ext_from=PL&index=85&playnext=1.

9 **"The reason people don't have health insurance"** Paul Krugman, "Mandates and Mudslinging," *New York Times*, November 30, 2007.

10 **Obama Democrats stayed home** The *New York Times* reported: "In President Obama's strongest areas—towns where he received more than 60 percent of the vote—the number of voters was about 30 percent below 2008 levels." http://www.nytimes.com/inter active/2010/01/19/us/politics/massachusetts-election-map.html.

11 **saved California motorists more than $62 billion on their premiums** J. Robert Hunter, *State Automobile Insurance Regulation: A National Quality Assessment and In-Depth Review of California's Uniquely Effective Regulatory System*, (Consumer Federation of America, April 2008). Download the report at http://www.consumerfed.org/elements/ www.consumerfed.org/file/finance/state_auto_insurance_report.pdf.

12 **The campaign for California Proposition 103** For the full history, read Harvey Rosenfield, "Auto Insurance: Crisis and Reform," *The University of Memphis Law Review* 29, no. 1 (Fall 1998).

12 **delivered $1.43 billion in refund checks** California Department of Insurance, 2006 Annual Report of the Insurance Commissioner, "Total refunds including interest for 149 companies/groups amounted to approximately $1.43 billion."

Chapter 2: Ten Rules of Populist Power

15 **"Positive Thoughts Regarding the Eight Hour Discharge"** Robin Abcarian, "Is 48 Hours So Much to Ask?" *Los Angeles Times*, May 15, 1996.

18 **Think Paul Revere** Malcolm Gladwell, *The Tipping Point* (New York: Little, Brown and Company, 2000).

19 **George Joseph is one of the four hundred**   http://www.forbes
.com/lists/2005/54/6RNR.html.

30 **"The industry has its advertising too, but far more effective"**   Brooks Jackson, "Doctors Make Washington House Call to
Support HMO Reform," CNN *Inside Politics*, July 23, 1998.

30 **"Dana vs. Goliath"**   "Payment Due" PBS *NOW,* May 6, 2006,
http://www.pbs.org/now/politics/050506_index.html#.

32 **"Their job is to implement my vision."**   Robert Gunnison,
"Davis Says He Calls All the Shots," *San Francisco Chronicle*, July 21,
1999. In the article he takes a shot at Ralph Nader, whom we had send
a letter to Davis.

34 **The Rx Express train trips**   Read more at http://www.rxexpress
canada.org/. Watch a documentary on the Rx Express at http://
www.youtube.com/consumerwatchdog#p/u/38/2dOYC9grLl4
(part 1) and at http://www.youtube.com/consumerwatchdog#p/u/
37/OO0bVb5hqfk (part 2).

42 **The California senate insurance committee, May 2003**
KRON-TV4, "Is State Senator Don Perata on the Take?" August
27, 2002, http://www.consumerwatchdog.org/insurance/
articles/?storyId=15186. The full history of the legislative assault
is available at http://www.consumerwatchdog.org/insurance/
articles/?storyId=29076

42 **The *Los Angeles Times* reported my ejection the next
day**   Virginia Ellis, "Insurer Uses Its Muscle on 2 Bills," *Los Angeles
Times*, May 8, 2003. *Los Angeles Times* editorial, "The Term Limits
Disaster: Cashing in at the Capitol," May 9, 2003. The editorial read:
"Legislators obviously know how bad this looks. During the Senate
hearing, consumer activist Jamie Court questioned whether Perata's
bill was about good policy or helping a company that happened
to give generously and broadly to members of the Legislature. 'Mr.
Court, you're done,' snapped committee Chairwoman Jackie Speier
(D-Hillsborough). A staffer took the microphone and Court was
escorted to the back of the small room, packed tightly with insurance
industry representatives. Perata huffed and puffed in outrage and insult.
The question is whether the lawmakers are embarrassed enough now to
kill both these bad bills."

43 **Perata subsequently came under FBI investigation**   The investigation was ultimately dropped. This news article recounts much of its
substance: Tim Reiterman, "Probe of Perata Dealings Quiet, But Alive,"
Los Angeles Times, November 4, 2007.

43 **Mercury Insurance received a subpoena** Christian Berthelson, "Obscure Political Group Linked to Perata," *San Francisco Chronicle*, November 24, 2004, http://www.sfgate.com/cgi-bin/article.cgi?file=/c/a/2004/11/24/MNGDHA0PPK1.DTL. "Joseph offered few details about the partnership in which he has an interest that received a subpoena in the Perata probe. Though the partnership has made political contributions on the state and federal level, he said the subpoena sought records related to its business dealings, not its political activity."

Chapter 3: Rousing Public Opinion in a New Media Age

44 **More Americans visit Twitter every month** The number was 29 million Americans per month in August 2009, a peak, with an average of 23 million Americans visiting per month. See Quantscore.com for the latest data.

44 **Monthly traffic on Facebook** It's the second most trafficked Web site in America, with 117 million individual Americans visiting each month. See Quantscore.com for the latest data.

45 **Ed Frawley's narrated montage** http://www.youtube.com/watch?v=46vYZFU1Dew.

46 **racist remark captured on video** http://www.youtube.com/watch?v=r90z0PMnKwI.

47 **an "accidential activist"** Alternet, "MoveOn As Instrument of the People," June 25, 2004, http://www.alternet.org/story/19043.

53 **"Technology enables insurgency"** Author interview, May 2010.

53 **"As supporters started to join MyBo"** Brian Stelter, "The Facebooker Who Friended Obama," *New York Times,* July 7, 2008.

57 **Half of the top twenty Web sites in America** They are Facebook, Twitter, eBay, Wikipedia, Blogger, Wordpress, MySpace, YouTube, Craigslist, and LinkedIn. In 2005, only two of these sites were in the top twenty most trafficked Web sites in America—MySpace.com and eBay.

Chapter 4: Building Your Own Populist 2.0 Platform

60 **Zuniga says, "To create long-lasting change"** Markos Moulitsas Zuniga, *Taking on the System: Rules for Radical Change in a Digital Era* (New York: Celebra Penguin, 2008), p. 11.

62 **Yedinsky offers the following** Author interview, May 2010.

66 **flash mob production** "Don't Get Caught in a Bad Hotel." Watch it at http://www.youtube.com/watch?v=-79pX1IOqPU.

67 **our campaign against Google** For the archive and ongoing drama visit our new Web site, http://www.insidegoogle.com.

Chapter 5: Getting the Affordable Health Care You Voted For

76 **Table 7, Americans on American Health Care**   Public opinion data from Henry Kaiser Family Foundation, site health08.org. The years 1991 and 2007 (leading up to the 1992 and 2008 elections) represent the two highest peaks of public disgust and disillusionment with the health care system; 42 percent of those polled in 1991, and 38 percent of those in 2007, when asked to assess U.S. health care, felt strongly enough about the drastic need for reform to go as far as to say that the system needed to be entirely abandoned and rebuilt. Likewise, only 6 percent and 11 percent of Americans, in those two years respectively, felt that the system adequately served their needs so as to merit only minor alterations, and 50 percent in both years felt fundamental changes needed to be made to improve salient flaws in the current health care administration.

Unfortunately, Americans' assessment, both in 1992 and currently, of the state of health care proves to be extremely apt. As recorded by the U.S. Census Bureau, approximately 15.8 percent of the American population in 2006 (the most recent year the study was conducted) still lacked any form of health insurance, a number that represents a 2 percent increase from the 13.8 percent of all Americans uninsured in 1992 (http://query.nytimes.com/gst/fullpage.html?res=9D0CE5DC16 30F93AA25751C1A967958260&sec=&spon=&pagewanted=2). Sadly, as the country's population has increased at a rapid rate (from 252 million in 1992 to 304 million in 2008), so too has the population of uninsured Americans followed more than proportionally (from 37.4 million to 47 million), a disheartening trend and result by any measurement (http://www.pnhp.org/news/2000/september/despite_economic_boo.php).

Consumer Reports found that 29 percent of those Americans with health insurance are considered underinsured, meaning their health care coverage does not cover their astronomically high costs. ("Are You Really Covered? Why 4 in 10 Americans Can't Depend On Their Health Insurance," Consumer Reports, September 2007, http://www.consumerreports.org/health/insurance/health-insurance-9-07/overview/0709_health_ov.htm).

78 **Workers with health insurance from an employer**   Milliman study in Kaiser Health News, May 15, 2008.

79 **2008 poll by my consumer group**   Campaign for Consumer Rights poll, January 2008, http://www.campaignforconsumerrights.org/archive/.

81 **only 16 percent supported the notion** National poll conducted December 4–7, 2008, by Consumer Watchdog, http://www .consumerwatchdog.org/patients/articles/?storyId=24110.

85 **PBS's *Bill Moyers Journal*** July 31, 2009, http://www.pbs.org/ moyers/journal/07312009/profile.html.

86 ***Dateline* aired its hour-long episode** January 24, 2010, http:// www.msnbc.msn.com/id/21134540/vp/35035291#35035291.

87 **"I think a company does have a right to make sure"** Lisa Girion, "Health Insurers Refuse to Limit Rescission of Coverage," *Los Angeles Times,* June 17, 2009.

89 **States have the ability to enact public options** States can enact public options, such as health insurance exchanges that bypass insurers, but under the federal law they will have to wait until 2017 before being able to tap into Medicare and Medicaid payments for subsidies to those who cannot afford to pay for coverage through a public option.

93 **Taxpayers and individuals got it in the shorts** Small businesses have also felt the pain of premium increases of up to 32 percent. These price hikes have forced Massachusetts to deal with cost directly. In the spring of 2010, Massachusetts's insurance commissioner issued emergency rules requiring health insurers to justify small-business premium increases and rejected 235 proposed increases as excessive and unreasonable. The state senate recently approved legislation that would require prior approval of all health premium increases, and that insurers spend at least 90 percent of premiums on medical care.

93 **12 to 33 percent of every premium dollar** Medical loss ratios as reported to California Department of Managed Health Care and by companies to Securities Exchange Commission.

96 **World Health Organization ranks the United States** 2000 was the last year the WHO did such a ranking after blowback from the United States. http://www.who.int/whr/2000/media_centre/press _release/en/index.html.

99 **"If you're starting from scratch"** Larissa MacFarquhar, "The Conciliator," *The New Yorker,* May 7, 2007.

99 **"So what I believe is we should set up a series of choices"** http://iowa.barackobama.com/page/community/tag/Ames.

100 **One hundred and thirty-two million Americans** Employee Benefits Research Institute, "ERISA Pre-Emptions: Implications for Health Reform and Coverage," February 2008. Number of workers and dependents in self-funded plans (partial or total): 73 million. Number in other private employer plans: 59.8 million. Number of workers and dependents covered by public employee plans: 27 million.

100 **the Supreme Court ruled in** *Pilot Life v. Dedeaux*   Read more
about the ramifications at http://www.makingakilling.org/chapter5
.html

102 **when I heard in the spring of 2009**   The White House confirmed
the deal in August 2009. David Patrick, "White House Affirms Deal
on Drug Cost," *New York Times*, August 5, 2009. See also Bob Herbert,
"This Is Reform," *New York Times*, August 17, 2009.

102 **Obama said he would haul the pharmaceutical execu-**
tives   Transcript from Barack Obama speech at Thaddeus Stevens
College of Technology Center in Lancaster, Pennsylvania, March 31,
2008, as seen on YouTube, http://www.youtube.com/watch?v=yE2vVc
0tN3Y&feature=related and http://www.youtube.com/watch?v=Tq4L
xHmhDmo&feature=related

(Starts at 8:00) "Within the first couple of months of me being
elected, we're going to call together a big meeting. We're going to have
a big round table and I'm going to invite everybody in. Insurance and
drug companies will have a seat at the table, they just won't be able to
buy it. And I'll sit at the table, I'll sit at the table, but I'll have the biggest
chair. . . . I want to listen to them. But here's the difference. I'm going to
do it all on C-SPAN [applause] so that the American people will know
what's going on, and so if you have some member of Congress who's
carrying water for the drug companies, saying 'Well, we can't negotiate for the cheapest available price on drugs, because all of these drug
companies need all of these profits in order to invest in research and
development,' well I'll be able to call in my health care expert in front
of national television and ask them, 'Is that true?' What he'll say is 'Well,
the drug companies do need some profits to reinvest in research and
development, but also, research and development is done by taxpayer
money . . . and a lot of what the drug companies call research and development is actually marketing costs for these TV ads where people are
running through fields looking all happy. . . .'"

103 **prescription drug costs are about 10 percent of health**
care expenses   Kaiser Family Foundation, http://www.kff.org/
rxdrugs/3057.cfm.

Chapter 6: Taming Arnold: A Blueprint for Confronting the Audacity of Phony Change

105 **"I will go to Sacramento and I will clean house."** Gary Delsoh
and Sam Stanton, "Day Of Surprises: Democrat Bustamante to Join
Race, Break Ranks," *Sacramento Bee*, August 7, 2003.

105 **"Any of those kinds of real big, powerful special interests"**
John Marelius, "Contradictions Abound for Schwarzenegger," *San Diego
Union Tribune,* August 31, 2003.

105 **"It is inherently suspect"**   Remaining quotes from http://www
.joinarnold.com/. See the rejoinder to them at http://www
.arnoldwatch.org/political_reform/index.php.

105 **more campaign cash than any politician**   The total was
$129,850,204 through December 2009: http://www.arnoldwatch
.org/special_interests/index.html. All contribution totals come from
the California secretary of state Web site and were chronicled at
ArnoldWatch.org based on the political committees controlled by
Schwarzenegger.

106 **Schwarzenegger claimed that the definition of "special interest"**   For example, see John Marelius, "Contradictions Abound for
Schwarzenegger," *San Diego Union Tribune*, August 31, 2003. Marelius
reports, "In a recent radio interview, Schwarzenegger drew a distinc-
tion between corporations that support him and the labor unions and
Indian tribes that are donating large sums to Davis and Lt. Gov. Cruz
Bustamante, the leading Democrat on the recall ballot. 'Any of those
kinds of real big, powerful special interests, if you take money from
them, you owe them something,' he said last week on Sacramento radio
station KTKX. Schwarzenegger stood by the contention throughout his
campaign and much of his first term.

107 **"I am a salesman by nature"**   He made the statement in his first
state of the state speech in January 2004.

109 **our Arnold Watch project had exposed the contradictions**   The
complete index is at http://www.arnoldwatch.org/blogs/index.php.

112 **this initiative was withdrawn**   Schwarzenegger later adopted
support for another initiative, Proposition 73, which would have
required parental consent for abortions and undermined Roe v. Wade
by redefining abortion as "death of an unborn child." He lost all
five initiatives on election night. For more details see http://www
.electionwatchdog.org/recommendations/

114 **After his defeat, Schwarzenegger reportedly told Senator Ted
Kennedy**   The information came to us from a political consultant
who claimed to have received the information from Kennedy.

117 **With a video camera rolling, we snuck into the ballroom**   Watch the video at http://arnoldwatch.org/assets/AW_mov/
century_sit.mov.

120 **Connie Bruck quoted weightlifter friend Franco
Columbu**   Connie Bruck, Letter from California, "Supermoderate!"
New Yorker, June 28, 2004, p. 68

122 **"You don't win many fights with nurses."**   Jack Pitney quoted in
Mark Martin, Carla Marinucci, and Lynda Gledhill, "Californians Say
No to Schwarzenegger," *San Francisco Chronicle*, November 5, 2005.

125 **"Flip-flopping is getting a bad rap"**   ABC's *This Week*, July 20, 2008.

Chapter 7: Direct Democracy: Using the Ballot Measure to Get the Change You Want

128 **a rare confluence of forces**   For the full story read Harvey Rosenfield, "Auto Insurance: Crisis and Reform," *The University of Memphis Law Review* 29, no. 1 (Fall 1998).

128 **a $63.8 million insurance-industry opposition campaign**   Kenneth Reich, "Insurance Fight Cost Initiative Backers at Total of $83 Million," *Los Angeles Times*, February 7, 1989.

129 **twenty-four states plus the District of Columbia**   For more details on the process in each visit the Ballot Initiative Strategy Center www.ballot.org.

136 **heartbreaking ballot fight in 2004**   It was for California Proposition 64.

Chapter 8: The Road to Cheaper and Cleaner Energy

145 **my consumer group tracked how gasoline prices fell**   Foundation for Taxpayer and Consumer Rights press release, "Investors, Like Consumers, See Politics in Pre-Election Oil and Gas Pricing," November 1, 2006, http://www.consumerwatchdog.org/energy/articles/?storyId=15182.

148 **oil companies cheat together to withhold needed gasoline**   Internal oil-industry memos show how oil companies have had a long-term strategic plan to keep the American gasoline supply from satisfying the public's demand for gasoline. Confidential memos from Mobil, Chevron, and Texaco reveal the different ways the oil giants closed down refining capacity and drove independent refiners out of business since the mid-1990s. The memos, made public by U.S. senator Ron Wyden and propelled by Consumer Watchdog, demonstrate a nationwide effort by the American Petroleum Institute (API), the lobbying and research arm of the oil industry, to encourage the major refiners to shutter refineries in the mid-1990s in order to raise the price at the pump. Read the memos at http://www.oilwatchdog.org/articles/?storyId=4018&topicId=8059&topicId=8070&archive=20.

148 **documented by government agencies like the Federal Trade Commission**   Melita Marie Garza, "Fuel Firms Cleared in Midwest Price Rise," *Chicago Tribune*, March 31, 2001. "Some oil companies reaped big profits by withholding supplies during last summer's Midwest gasoline crunch, but overall the industry was cleared of colluding to raise prices, according to a government report released Friday . . . the report

said there were 'conscious [but independent] choices by industry partici-
pants' to engage in profit-maximizing strategies." The article refers to the
Final Report of the Federal Trade Commission, "Midwest Gasoline Price
Investigation," March 29, 2001.

148 **Over the last twenty years, America's demand for gasoline** Jad
Mouawad, "Storm Stretches Refiners Past a Perilous Point," *New York
Times* September 11, 2005. Also see the accompanying graphic "Trying
to Keep Up with Demand."

152 **Judy Dugan, a longtime journalist** "Road to Cleaner and
Cheaper," Consumer Watchdog, May 19, 2009, http://www.oilwatch-
dog.org/articles/?storyId=27389.

154 **San Diego, which was the first region to fully deregulate** Foundation for Taxpayer and Consumer Rights Report, "Hoax:
How Deregulation Let the Power Industry Steal $71 Billion from
California," January 17, 2002, p. 6; Greg LaMotte, "San Diego at Center
of California Deregulation Dispute," CNN.com, December 20, 2000.

154 **However, defying the economic logic proposed** According to
the California Independent System Operator (the state's grid manager),
compared to 1999 peak demand was down 5 percent in July 2000 and
down 1 percent in August 2000.

155 **By 2001, the $23 billion of bad corporate debt** From monthly
and annual transition cost filings with the California Public Utilities
Commission for PG&E and Southern California Edison, as compiled by
the Utility Reform Network.

155 **Workers at one of these power plants later testified** Kevin
Yamamura and Emily Bazar, "Employees: Power Supply Held Down,"
Sacramento Bee, June 22, 2001.

155 **On some temperate December days the price of energy** "June
11, 2001, Monthly Calendar of Daily Maximum Prices," Consortium
for Electric Reliability Technology Solutions (CERTS) Market Pricing
Resource Site, Updated. CERTS monitors the reliability of the U.S.
electric power system.

156 **According to the Credit Suisse analyst** Credit Suisse/First
Boston, Paul Patterson, analyst, "US Economics Comment: A Very Brief
Note on California," January 18, 2001. Miguel Bustillo, "Wall Street
Firm's Web Site Calls Blackouts a Tactic to Raise Rates," *Los Angeles
Times,* January 15, 2001.

Chapter 9: Bringing Wall Street Back Under Control

165 **$80 million in campaign contributions** Center for Responsible
Politics, http://www.opensecrets.org.

165 **egged on by their pollsters, like Frank Luntz**   Memo by Dr. Frank Luntz, "The Language of Financial Reform," Word Doctors, January 2010.

165 **armed with ammo from their own public-opinion prognosticators**   Memo by Celinda Lake, "Response to Frank Luntz memo on Financial Reform," Lake Research Partners, February 22, 2010.

166 **Securities and investment firms gave 69 percent**   Data from Center for Responsible Politics, http://www.opensecrets.org.

173 **This system has allowed Consumer Watchdog**   See the list of intervenor actions leading to the savings at http://www.consumer watchdog.org/images/InsSavings.gif.

Chapter 10: Stopping the Wars and Reinvesting in America

180 **"Now, eight months later, we're being presented"**   http://www .lorettasanchez.house.gov/index.php?option=com_content&task=view &id=674&Itemid=79

180 **Hundreds of thousands suffered from post-traumatic stress disorder**   Bob Herbert, "War, Endless Wards," *New York Times,* March 2, 2009, http://www.nytimes.com/2009/03/03/opinion/03herbert.html?s cp=13&sq=bob+herbert+and+afghanistan&st=nyt.

184 **National Priorities Project has compiled an analysis**   http:// www.nationalpriorities.org/costofwar_home.